Innovative Business Models

Innovative Business Models

Disruptive Strategies for the Modern Entrepreneur

Alex Wealthfield

Mindful Pages

Published in 2024

ISBN: 9789362926357 (PB)
ISBN: 9789362920898 (eBook)

Published by

Mindful Pages
Imprint of Alpha Editions LLC
312 W. 2nd St #1834
Casper, WY 82601, USA
www.mindfulpagespublishers.com

Contents

Introduction

The business environment of today is a dynamic and complex environment that is shaped by the rapid development of modern technologies, the continuously changing demands of the target customer, and the growing connectivity of local markets into one global market. It is not the era, when business could survive just by using the same business practices and improve them slowly; in today's world, every company that wants to survive and succeed should be rapid in its adaptation to the change and innovative in its ways. The major factor shaping the current business environment is the digital revolution. The development of the internet, mobile technologies, and cloud computing services has changed the business landscape forever. This change has been mainly due to the blurring of industry lines and introduction of new companies into the markets where such giants as Sony, Walmart, and others used to be the only and undisputed leaders. In the retail market, these were the companies like Amazon and Alibaba that revolutionized the industry by obtaining all the data about the preferences of the clients, using the artificial intelligence to create a demand for the products that has not existed before, and using the most effective logistics. In the media market, the leaders of today that are introduced as the new companies are Netflix and others that use the changing habits of the customers in every corner of the world to provide the on-demand streaming services to the customers, fulfilling the role of TV stations and main media sources in one. The list could go on, and the truth is that digital technologies have changed the business landscape in a way that provides every company on a global basis access to new sources of revenue, ways of optimization of company processes, and ways of gaining insights into the customer behavior.

In addition, the expectations of customers have changed dramatically. Today's consumer is the most well-informed, interconnected, and granted of any other in the entire history. Their needs for convenience, speed, and customization are at their peak due to the opportunities to have everything they want right here, right now. The example of Apple, Google, and Tesla companies demonstrates that people are ready to pay more for getting those things that they have never expected. In this situation, the emergence of this feature has made many businesses revise their approaches to work focusing on an offer of not something else but an experience. The second reason that differentiates the modern business environment is a fast-growing interest in all things sustainable and responsible. Today's world is aware of numerous issues and things about the environment and the needs of social justice. People become more and more interested in proving their engagement in the resolution of these problems. Many companies have to follow this tendency and switch to sustainable work. It occurs in many industries, from the food sector to the clothing one. Brands like Patagonia and Tesla have impacted the way of work make other companies and prove that caring for the environment can be not just vital but profitable. Finally, the emergence of the ESG as a significant criterion for investing has made s sustainable core of business and a long-term course on this sphere a must for businesses that are going to succeed.

The surrounding world has altered in a drastic fashion, so has the way businesses coexist with a variety of competing firms. The majority of industries have become more amalgamated and less separate in the present day. Companies of different types and industries are compelled to compete for the same set of customers. The blurring of the lines is especially prevalent in technology-driven industries, where data and powerful digital platforms make it much easier for companies to transition from their original industry. Tech corporations like Amazon, Google, or Apple do not merely do e-commerce, feature search engines or sell devices anymore. They also specialize in healthcare, finance, automotive, and many other industries without consideration of the type of product they work with. Such a situation suggests critical changes to the unique innovations of a company, as the latter do not compete uniquely with the regular industry and must compete against other companies in alien industries. Moreover, globalization is another challenge to innovation, as the latter is forced to adapt to the whole new scale of competition. On the one hand, companies have a broader pool of customers, new markets, and international suppliers. On the other hand, the regulatory challenges and geo-political risks require a substantial amount of assets to assist with managing a global scale of operations. In addition, there is an increased risk of competition from established international companies as well as international startups. Finally, the surge of e-commerce allows any business to have an international dimension to its operations, while also raising the bar of competition in terms of customer expectations.

The chief feature of the modern business environment is the rapid pace of change. New products and markets are born and die in a matter of years, with technological advancements enabling companies to reach global markets in short order. In this situation, the businesses that succeed are those that innovate and adapt most effectively. Thus, a culture of continuous innovation should be adopted by all firms; it implies that innovation is not a one-time initiative or the responsibility of a single department – rather, it must be ingrained into every aspect of the firm's operations. Leaders must promote a culture of experimentation, where failure is not the end, but the beginning of a new cycle, and where the question of "how can we improve" is asked on a daily basis. The transformation of a company into an innovation-centric entity also requires investment in research and development, the establishment of cross-functional teams, and the development of an agile organization that can rapidly respond to market changes.

Equally important is the fact that innovation has become more collaborative in the modern era. It is a paradox of the current state of technological advancement that with so much knowledge, no single business has all the answers. Therefore, businesses and their leaders have come to understand the importance of partnerships and alliances, whether it be with other firms or with the start-up companies and consumers. Thus, within even the most competitive and conservative industries, open innovation models have become more and more common. In conclusion, in the world of rapid change, technological advancements, and heavy competition, innovation is not just a luxury, but a necessity. In order to become one of the hero businesses of the new era, firms and their leadership must focus on digitalization, reconsideration of their relationship with the customers, and collaboration.

To this, I need to note that the transformation is nowadays driven by disruptive business models. By this I do not mean the phenomenon that ride-sharing apps substitute the traditional taxi services. Rather, a disruptive business model changes the industry fundamentally, reshaping the customer experiences and altering the value production business logic. This, normally, happens when the newcomer offers a product or a service that would be a missed opportunity to take on by the incumbent player. Thus, the industry shifts from, for instance, software sales to a subscription system or offering a meal delivery as the main product for people in isolation emerged, etc. In our work, we will talk about the companies that managed to win the game of disruption, describing in detail how they effectively acted but also what risks they took. In the text we will analyze cases of these companies providing a new value proposition to be attractive to the customers, articulating the customer-centric logic, inventing the new ways of delivery – or any other work that is required to make a good business model a truly disruptive one. The book will be easy to read, and at the same time, it will provide a lot of helpful tools and tactics that can enable you to think disruptively and see the innovations that your competitors have missed. Making a strong emphasis on the practical dimension, I will show many real-case examples of such disruptive business models. The book should be useful for entrepreneurs willing to start a new business, corporate executives as well as the readers who want to know how this very moment the industries are being reshaped.

Reading this book, and the chapters that follow, will help you to understand the current business environment and appreciate that disruption is not a phase that we are going through. It is the status quo. You will learn how to predict when change will occur and how to manage it. And you will uncover the secrets of forging your own disruptive strategy, which will enable you to be the market leader in your sphere. From reading which great companies succeeded where others failed and how to develop a culture of innovation unwittingly, you will be alight to the practices that will see you not just survive, but thrive, in an ever-shifting world.

Chapter 1: Understanding Disruption in Business

The movement of business models is a proof of the adaptiveness of commerce and industry. Over the years, businesses have been shifting. From traditional, linear models to more innovative, fluid models that meet the demands of today's complex commercial phenomena. This shift has been influenced by the development of technology, purchasing behavior, as well as the pressure exerted on businesses by the global economy. To understand how businesses function in this day and age, we have to look into the question of how traditional business models were replaced by the innovative approaches that are currently found and used throughout the business world that are widely-used nowadays. In the past, business models were quite simple and limiting for those who practiced it. For centuries, it was suitable for businesses and depended on a rigid system and structure. Interestingly, it was in the early industrial era when businesses managed to shift their inside functionality and organization. Namely, companies began operating in a hierarchical top-down order, where the process of decision making was centralized. There were not that many goods to sell. As a result, companies were operating on a product-centric basis. Focusing on production, businesses were interested in bargaining. Companies tried to sharpen the product into good investigating lifetime. They streamlined the production process and produced in masses to save costs because the bigger the lot the cheaper the thing. Accordingly, the production created a volume. Thus, the distribution process included familiar or newly-accepted business. Success was determined through the company's ability to cavil its production capacity and the product it managed to place on the market that also maintained a credible quality, but the lowest price.

Perhaps, one of the first and most well-known representation of a standard business model is the assembly line invented by Henry Ford. Henry Ford managed to develop an innovative mass production model due to breaking the long and complicated production process into smaller parts. Subsequently, when workers were hired they did not have to be skilled in everything, but only to complete one simple task. As a result, the need to adjust to a different process was eliminated. Thanks to this innovative model, Ford succeeded in producing the Model T in the early twentieth century. To achieve higher production scales, they tried controlling costs, which was essential to produce a single unit of the Model T at tens of dollars. Thus, Ford managed to reduce the vehicle's cost making it accessible to a larger number of consumers. It should be noted that this model then began to be used by a multitude of businesses that aimed to be effective by producing as much as possible in the shortest time and minimize production costs.

Traditional business models, such as Ford's, dominated industries for much of the 20th century. Success was defined by a company's ability to expand and grow. The era was characterized by large corporations that controlled the production, distribution, and supply chains of their products. This was an age of vertical integration in which each company tried to do everything in-house. Although effective at producing high rates of efficiency in a non-competitive environment, these institutions mutually held monopolies and oligopolies in their designated industries . Ultimately, they failed to secure their place in the market due to their inefficiency and inflexibility. By the end of the 20th century, models that had succeeded for almost 100 years were rapidly falling by the wayside due to competition and choice. The demise of traditional models and their departure from the market were due to the shifting of approaches to a firm-centric perspective. When businesses first began to digitize, a world of possibility existed for creating new ways of doing things. Firms began data mining, processing, and analyzing their data on a scale never previously imagined. The new approach focused both on customers and customers' needs as opposed to just products. Therefore, instead of commodities, delivery needs to consider how firms deliver value to customers. This has driven the market toward a more efficient, customized approach to servicing the customer.

One of the most defining shifts in business models came with the advent of the internet in the 1990s. It radically changed the way companies could do business, allowing them to operate on a global scale with minimal investment. E-commerce emerged as a new business model for companies such as Amazon, eBay, Alibaba, and many others, which provided customers with direct access to any product while establishing themselves as mere intermediaries between the buyers and the producers. Obviously, the advantages of this scheme – from lower prices to better selection and convenience – showed that this was a way of the future, while many traditional brick-and mortar enterprises became obsolete. However, the prominence of e-commerce led to the emergence of another business model – that of a platform. Unlike intermediaries, platforms manage an ecosystem that connects producers and consumers of goods and services; such classic examples as Uber, Airbnb, or even Facebook are highly scalable and make money from the transactions between the users of their services – whether these be transport, accommodation, or social communication. Meanwhile, the increasingly digital nature of the world beyond business created more opportunities for new revenue models. The subscription model, at first a product of the rise of software and cloud computing, paradoxically, is a non-deceptively simple swap of customer relations; instead of making a single purchase, customers are only granted a lease of the product, meaning that the company who provides the service must continually provide value to the customer. Software-as-a-Service such as Salesforce, Adobe, or Microsoft, have used this model to great effect, while it quickly became prominent in other sectors like entertainment via Netflix or Spotify, or personal care via providers such as Dollar Shave Club.

Moreover, the transition to innovation was realized along with the changes in business strategies that are now oriented on sustainability and corporate social responsibility. Due to the fact that customers are becoming more and more concerned about environmental and social issues, business models have changed regarding their attitudes to these problems. The linear models of taking away, making, and disposing of goods have been substituted for circular business models, which are focused on the reusing of resources, high efficiency of these resources, and low waste levels. Patagonia and IKEA are one of the companies that are leading this trend and implementing these sustainable trends in their core businesses by promoting the longevity of their production, recycling goods, and responsible sourcing. In addition, the modern business world is also focused on the trends of personalization and customization. In the digital age, when companies have the necessary tools and data about their customers to analyze and personalize their experiences, they try to implement this trend in almost all business areas. For example, the world of fashion and digital technologies, including companies such as Nike, Apple, and Amazon, are using the data to be able to provide highly personalized offers, knowledge of customer needs, desires, and ability to react to it with tailored products. In a highly competitive environment, a skill of personalization is one of the essential advantages of the companies that customers use to choose their products. Finally, one of the effects of modern business transformation is the shift toward more innovative organizations. The main difference between old and modern organizations is the rigidness of the old one, which is slow, has a lot of rules, a hierarchy, and inflexible with the outer environment. In contrast, modern innovative companies are associated with agility and decentralization, for instance, by adopting flat structures that are common among startups that prioritize creativity, initiative, and response to the market.

In conclusion, the evolution of business models from traditional to innovative can be regarded as a symbol of the general process of adaptation to new conditions, which is especially relevant in a rapidly changing and highly volatile environment. While the traditional model was focused on efficiency, standardization, and control, the modern-day approach is more oriented on the rapid change and is centered around flexibility, sustainability, and innovation as the primary values. As the world of business continues to evolve rapidly, companies should follow the evolved trends and remain flexible and change-oriented since it is the key to success in the present environment. The future of business belongs to companies that would not just monitor but rather create the six of value.

Key concepts of disruption: What it means and why it matters

The concept of disruption has become incredibly important in the business world. Disruption changes how we think about competition, innovation, and the ways in which the markets function. At its core, a disruption is a process through which a smaller and less resourceful company is able to successfully challenge an industry's incumbent leader. Disruptors typically begin by targeting a part of the targeted market that is undershot by the leading company, optimizing their product to be easier to use, cheaper, or more convenient. As the disruptors improve and expand their market, they ascend through the ranks, eventually overthrowing the industry's leaders. Learning about these concepts might be invaluable for many modern companies that need to find their place on a rapidly changing market, as it allows understanding how new technologies and business practices reshape entire industries.

The term is attributed to Clayton Christensen, and it was made publically known in his book, The Innovator's Dilemma. The key concepts are those of sustaining and disruptive innovations. According to Christensen, established companies stay on the market by providing sustaining innovations to their customer base, making their products better and their consumption more enjoyable. However, in doing so, they direct their attention on the people who comprise the company's most prominent and profitable consumers. In the process, the benefits that the products provide to less profitable, vital, and sometimes underserved customers are overlooked. Smaller companies are able to optimally assess the deficiencies of the established companies, and provide innovations that, while appearing to be worse than the market leaders' offerings at first glance, optimally serve the neglected customers. Eventually, these innovations provide more and more benefits, and the products ascend the market, forcing the incumbent companies out.

Disruption is crucial for industries because it has the potential to force established companies to take steps toward evolution. Over time, market leaders in prominent industries often become used to their processes and dominant market position, thereby failing to see the need for major business model revisions to improve value creation for their customers. Incumbents often mine their most profitable customers for any available spending and then focus on providing an ever-improving experience for that segment. However, while the small, incremental improvements incumbent companies make over time are effective in the short run, they can be problematic in the long term. Such companies can struggle to differentiate between useful trends, such as changing customer demand, and existing business models that already satisfy most customers adequately. As such, industries stagnate, and there is no incentive to improve either their value creation or the experience of their customers.

Disruptors can do entirely without any significant changes if they are able to take a minimalist, affordable, and accessible approach to market saturation. Such companies target the majority of the market that the incumbent companies do not see as their target audience, infuse them with added utility, and ensure that they can properly satisfy their needs from the start. While the disruptor's products and services are not likely to be sufficiently advanced to satisfy the need of the highest-end customers at the start of their market presence, they improve their offerings over time, and it gradually becomes more difficult to distinguish between the custodians of the current model and the disruptors. Once the improvements of the disruptive technology reach the level where they can match the needs of the mainstream customers, the former exceed the incumbents and displace them from their positions.

The first reason why disruption matters is its increased frequency and effectiveness. With the rise of digital technology, disruption has become more common and intense in the recent past. As explained by Christensen, the digital platforms have enabled many new entrepreneurs and start-up companies to reach their customers, develop their brands, and scale up their ideas. For instance, Airbnb fostered peer-to-peer accommodation-sharing using digital technology, yet it did not introduce any innovative technology. However, this created an alternative and cheaper way of accessing entire apartments or rooms, disrupting the hotel industry. In addition, the creation of industry online platforms on the internet has also provided an opportunity to develop a business newly in different ways. Take, for example, when Uber and Lyft disrupted the transportation industry by enabling people to share rides using mobile apps directly. The main takeaway is that the easy access allowed competition to develop new ideas to make traditional services obsolete.

The second reason why disruption matters is that it can change the structure of an industry. In the past, many industries followed hierarchies that were easy to predict, and a few players remained dominant for several years. For instance, the hospitality industry was acquainted to 5-star level, 4-star, and three-star hotels and guesthouses. However, with the onset of Airbnb, 1-star homes can now be put on the market, and it is affordable. This kind of class did not exist in this industry before; this kind of industry's powerful ones were unable to predict the aspects of their offerings to make the sector profitable. The third reason is that sometimes it can entirely transform the structure of an industry. For instance, with the introduction of digital television, streaming services such as Netflix became paramount players in the entertainment industry. As a result, cable and other TV channels had to transform their industries to acquire the business in other ways of distributing their channels.

However, disruption is not necessarily a negative process. Although it often poses challenges, it also creates opportunities for growth and development. Disruptive changes for companies that are willing to accept them can be a reward. In some cases, incumbents not only defended their position but also continued to develop profitable investments. Realizing the threat of disruption, a number of incumbents managed to transform their business models or absorb the innovators. As a result, they retained or even increased their market share. For example, it is possible to note that Microsoft, which was considered a slow giant for several years, is successfully transforming. The company quickly switched to the development of cloud computing and focused on offering the Azure cloud service. Today, Microsoft has finally taken its place in the new world of rapid spinning forces of market destruction. It gained success partly because the company's management correctly read the tea leaves and reoriented the business, which meant much handwriting 10-15 years ago on the wall for the company in which the last decade smelled of decay or aging at best.

Overall, disruption should make one stop and think about the necessity of being customer-centric. The most important thing that made organizations successful was the focus on market demand. The innovators who achieved success did not compete with old market players for consumers, thinking up how to make their largely similar technologies better but created new technologies that provided real value where no one seemed to need it. This proves that understanding the client's ideas and processes and their satisfaction in new conditions, though not the most perfect and comfortable for the history of an enterprise or office, are essential if one wants to launch an innovation.

One of the challenges associated with the issue concerning the reaction of the incumbents to the disruption is the dilemma of the innovator. In other words, many companies are reliant on their existing business models, customer networks, and overall general organization. Even though the essence of the new technologies and approaches is perceived by large firms, their process is not easily undergone by incumbents in most cases. This is attributed to the activity's essential implication of sacrificing the existing products of companies in order to gain some entirely new one which, in the case of genuine disruption, is underdeveloped. It means that businesses' reliance on their most successful means for products and clients becomes the cause for which they are exposed to the so-called innovator's dilemma effectively. Large businesses avoid innovation on the basis that concentrating on their core products and clients is the most reasonable strategy for success. At the same time, they are susceptible to the low-end disruption, the key characteristic of which is its target fixation on the lower section of a market. In this connection, the innovator's dilemma is the paradox caused by a rigid concentration on extended formulations and the profiting of particular customer groups. Thus, the problem with the interaction of the incumbents and disruptors is such that the firms' attention to either external influence and substitution of the central target by newcomers or internal factors and concrete circumstances leads to losses.

"The times they are a-changing" – and have always been, apparently. In the end, disruption is not just a trend; it is a core of how industries change and transform due to new technologies and needs. It challenges existing players, changes the market condition, and progress businesses to innovations beyond mere improvements. In order to compete in modern markets, one has to understand disruption; indeed, such knowledge is key to taking advantage of disruption and mitigating challenges it might pose. In other words, the only constant in the era of ever-changing technologies, business and market demands is innovation and the ability to embrace it.

Characteristics of disruptive business models

Disruptive business models are uniquely constructed models that allow new businesses to compete with established industries. These models exploit unmet or underserved market needs and create unique ways to add value, whether it be at a lower cost, with greater convenience, or participate in a more enhanced customer-experience. Such models seem to be inferior to existing conditions but can be accommodated by existing leaders and make more established solutions obsolete when they scale and improve over the interest of mainstream customers. A defining characteristic of these models is that they always target customers overlooked by established models. Often developed to service markets that cannot afford existing prices or lack other distractions addressed by established businesses. Disruptive companies usually begin by serving niche customers. For example, in the early days of personal computing, disruptive companies such as Apple and Microsoft began selling personal computers. These computers are simpler and more affordable than the complex and expensive mainframe systems sold by IBM at the time. A hobbyist or small business that cannot afford expensive machines will be the first to adopt these cheap and easy-to-use personal computers. Over time, the product will become better and better until it can be widely adopted and will eventually a replacement or disruptive solution in the vast market.

Cost reduction is another critical feature of disruptive business models. Usually, disruptors discover ways to deliver products or services at prices far lower than their competitors, making them more accessible for a broadened target group. In some cases, these improvements are based on new technologies that do not require costly equipment to be used. Sometimes such reductions are feasible due to eliminating intermediaries or optimizing business operations. In the latter case, disruptive companies may employ staff more effectively and require fewer workers due to online order placement. For instance, the concept of the sharing economy disrupted traditional businesses by enabling individuals to perform services for others. By doing so, consumers do not need to employ large corporations with numerous specialists, and workers do not need to bother about obtaining employment and sufficient payment. In their efforts to introduce such simplicity into the order process, Airbnb and Uber empowered common property owners, who are not real businessmen, to fulfill the needs of other people. As such, the growth of the sharing economy is one of the most vivid examples of both cost reduction and a focus on simplicity. In the same way, both companies are also representative of the ease-of-use approach since their services are not typically automated and require neither advanced technical skills nor complex preparation.

Thus, another major feature of disruptive business models is a relentless focus on simplicity and ease of use. While widespread customers of traditional companies need sophisticated and feature-rich solutions, there are many people striving to find as easy and simple solutions as possible. Typically, disruptors specifically target such customers making their offerings particularly appealing in terms of simplicity.

At least partly, disruptive business models are based on working with the help of new technologies. Very often, such technologies are either recently invented or not used to the full extent, which disruptors can introduce and popularize, if the technology is an existing one, or create and develop, if this is a totally new thing. In all cases, new technologies allow to develop new methods of interaction with the use of the digital tools, primarily it concerns using the Internet. Netflix is a good example of successfully using the new technologies for disrupting traditional industries. It used streaming technology and the possibility of watching movies and TV series on demand, without needing any disks, CD's, tapes, subscriptions, videos, etc. on another word, without any need to buy or distribute any physical products which can be very expensive. Netflix took advantage of wide-spread usage of the Internet and personal home computers and made a digital broadcasting of videos, and did it at a quite low price. Overall, the usage of digital technologies is a distinct characteristic of the disruptive business model, and many if not all successful disruptive business models might be at least partially digital. With the help of creative implementation of digital innovations, disruptors can develop new business models, which compete with the existing ones and are much more convenient and available.

Another characteristic is that any disruptive business model is very scalable. Traditional business models rely on large investments in infrastructure and supply chain and often in various physical assets from machines and computers to buildings. Instead, disruptors develop their business plans in a way that they can become easily scalable and not require large initial investment to create, as soon as they get access to the market. In many cases, this is achieved with the help of platforms or networks and so-called network effects, operation of which allows to increase the value of the service with every new user of the service. Facebook and many other social networks violated traditional communication and advertising system, making a platform, on which users post thoughts and pictures. The more people join the network, the more content there is the more reasons it all creates for people to join the network. In the result, Facebook has more than 2 billion active monthly users, and billions of people around the world were affected by the rise of social networking. This is indeed incredible performance for a business of any size, and it required at the starting point almost no investment in the infrastructure or supply chain.

Another critical feature of disruptive business models is their customer-centric nature. To be successful, disruptors should be able to recognize the gaps that are not addressed by the existing systems and create their offering. Such companies often address the needs of their target customers in a way not covered by the traditional businesses. Most often, they do it through the consideration of better customer experience, i.e., more personalized, convenient, or faster response. For instance, Amazon disrupted the retail industry by creating an online marketplace that was highly convenient for its customers as it allowed an in-depth customers' data analysis and personalized recommendations. Such a feature helps the company build customer loyalty, thus creating a profound gap between traditional retailers who were concentrated primarily on their products instead of customers' needs. Thus, with the customer being in the center of a disruptive business model, a focus on adjusting company strategies to the evolving customers' needs becomes a considerable gap with traditional businesses who are more focused on product improvement and product service augmentation than on the customer preparedness to buy the product.

Another crucial characteristic of explanatory business models is disruptors' ability to adapt and be open to change. As they do not always know the gaps that are not addressed by the system from the very start, successful disruptors are often initially based on some simple idea but remain open to change as they grow. This flexibility is essential as it allows these companies to pivot or broaden their focus relying on the existing evidence. As soon as a target market niche addresses a specific leverage able gap, successful disruptors strive to expand and dominate the larger market niche. For example, Tesla started by producing high-end electric vehicles for the customers who were environmentally conscious to thus be ready to pay a high price for a non-harmful product. Looking at the first results, the company soon used its key competency – the data received on how to produce electric vehicles and began producing more affordable versions and also created a global charging infrastructure, becoming thanks to that one of the leaders in automotive with a much larger market niche than initially targeted.

On top of all, disruptive business models differ from traditional ones by redefining existing industry's value chains. Instead of continuing with production, distribution, and delivery of goods or services following established patterns, disruptors introduce new logics. These might imply elimination of intermediaries, rearrangement of supply chains, or application of novel strategies to involving customers. For example, since time immemorial, prescription glasses were sold through opticians and retail shops. Owning a few large companies, these piles of few competitors were the only option available. However, Warby Parker launched a platform selling stylish and cheap glasses online. By removing intermediaries from the glasses-selling market and relying on a direct-to-the-customer method, this company disrupted the industry that was governed by a few large competitors.

To sum up, the key characteristics of disruptive business models differ them from traditional ones altogether. Targeting hitherto unattended markets, reducing costs, simplifying offerings, employing new technologies, being customer-centered and – at least potential – highly scalable, the disruptors diverge existing notions of value creation. Due to their highly adaptable nature, disruptive business models redefine existing industry's value chains, standing above them in these novel settings. As disruption is one of the key drivers of the contemporary economy, affecting market conditions, and leading companies to either innovate or disappear, it is vital for contemporary businesses to acknowledge the key characteristics of such models.

Case studies of early disruptors and their impact on industries

The notion of disruption is not new, but it is no secret that its frequency and consequences have significantly increased in a digital age. Different companies have turned out to be disruptors, reshaping entire industries, and changing market patterns in ways that were considered impossible. As a rule, customers appreciate any innovations made by new companies, as well as new or unique solutions to old problems. In the case of early disruptors, new companies often entered a market that was already filled with big players, and was capable of changing some industries. These main early disrupters can also be considered the "industry founders," who upon entering the market and actively changing it. Thus some of the best cases of this disruptive effect help one understand exactly how disruption worked, why it was successful, and in terms of whole industries, why it left a mark.

I can suggest that one of the most famous early disruptors was Ford Motor Company. At the beginning of the twentieth century, the automobile industry belonged to luxury car-makers, and cars themselves were a luxury item accessible primarily to reach people. Back at that time, cars were uncommon on city streets, and the forward-thinking Henry Ford managed to disrupt the industry by creating Model T, in 1908. A man was striving to make cars affordable to an average American who was denied an opportunity to buy a car. To reach this goal, Henry Ford managed to invent an assembly line – a revolutionary manufacturing process that drastically cut production costs. Dividing one complex task at the assembly of a car into little simple steps, Ford managed to drastically speed up the process and drop the cost of one car to way less than that of his competitors. Thus, the impact of Ford's disruption was unprecedented. The Model T was the first "people's car" that millions of middle-class people all around the world could purchase. Even today, a car is regarded as a primary means of transportation and is not a luxury item. It is also worth mention that assembly line methodologies have become adopted by companies all over the globe and in different industries as a way to better production efficiency and lower cost by applying some of Ford's solutions.

An earlier disruptor was Kodak and although it is an early example, its story does provide a lesson for the success and failure to adapt. In 1888, Kodak released the first mass-market camera, and enabled photography to be something the everyone could do. Before Kodak, photography was an expensive and difficult process, and was often conducted by professional photographers with the right camera equipment. Kodak disrupted the industry by producing, making a simple camera that anyone could use and developing and selling film. The business model included selling film and developing the photos, and notable its famous slogan was "you press the button, and we do the rest". Kodak rocked the established photography model by making the camera a simple process, enabling photography as a mass-market and not just a professional, and democratized what was an elite industry. The major company produced these cameras for over a century and used the process for much of their history. Kodak, who had developed one of the first digital cameras, failed to embrace the displacement of film and established photographic model by digital disruption; the shift meant that companies such Canon and Nikon and later the founder such as Samsung and Apple ruled the market and left Kodak struggling to switch from its main source of profitability. It can be learned that Kodak was successful with disruptive technology but failed, and thus we should constantly change with the industry constant of change.

Another early disruptor, IBM, had a significant impact on the transformation of the computing industry. Mid-20th century computers were large and expensive, and they were used almost exclusively by the government and large corporations . In 1953 IBM disrupted the computing industry by introducing the first commercially available computer, the IBM 650, designed specifically for business. While the vast majority of those early computers were difficult to use and required specific knowledge and specialization, IBM 650 was smaller, cheaper, and more user-friendly. It became a tool that a larger number of businesses could use. This invention was only the beginning of the commercialization of computing and paved the way for the development of personal computers that followed in the upcoming decades. IBM's disruption was arguably more significant, as it was instrumental in the transition of computers from a niche technology to an everyday tool for businesses. IBM continued to innovate in the coming years and made significant contributions to the development of mainframes, personal computers, and software. However, like Kodak, IBM itself became a victim of disruption, when in the 80s and 90s other companies, chiefly Microsoft and Apple, became the frontrunners of the personal computer revolution.

Southwest Airlines is one more early disruptor, who revolutionized the airline industry by the low-cost and no-frills business model. When Southwest was established in 1967, the airline industry was covered by major carriers offering complex, high-cost services, including meals, and complex routes. Southwest suddenly disrupted the industry with its philosophy of keeping things simple, affordable, and efficient. The airline applied a point-to-point routing system of transportation, which was not only quicker and more efficient in terms of turnaround time but also in terms of the flights' directionality. The company was able to avoid time wastage and offer cheaper tickets. As for the quality of the service, the airline decided to avoid some unnecessary services, such as in-flight meals or assigned seats, which also reduced the potential costs. Thus, it was possible for the company to provide a simple, but reliable service, at lower fares that attracted a big number of people, who were unable to buy expensive tickets. The consequence of the company's disruptive business model was that the established carriers were forced to rethink their ticket pricing, whereas a new low-cost carrier industry was obliged to be created. Nowadays, the low-cost carriers are an important part of the airline industry. The impact of Southwest Airlines is so huge, that its principles of doing business had to be taken into account by other airlines all over the world.

One of the most celebrated case studies in the history of business, Apple's disruption of the personal computing and consumer electronics industries has undoubtedly made a significant impact. Established in 1976, Apple primarily focused on producing personal computers, with its Apple II becoming one of the first mass-market personal computers to achieve any level of commercial success. To that effect, Apple's first major disruption took place in that time and was related to its technological innovations in the field. In the early 2000s, Apple produced what was its most significant disruption, namely the iPod, which was then followed by the introduction of the iPhone in 2007. Disrupting the mobile phone industry, the Apple phone has also had consequences on music, camera, and software industries. Its significance lay in the fact that 'it was the first to combine a phone, music player, camera, and internet browser in one device'. As such, Apple's introduction of the iPhone has transformed the relationship to technological and communicational devices, but its implications extended further. For example, the launch of the iPhone has defined the modern mobile app economy, as the first iPhone app store was released in 2008. At that, the disruption of the existing stationary mobile phone market had begun, with Nokia, Motorola, and Blackberry, which failed to adapt, being at this point practically irrelevant. With the iPhone, Apple has also managed to combine numerous technologies and eliminate limits in relation to whether particular smartphones were simply phones, cameras, music players, or personal computers.

Netflix is another great example of a company that disrupted an entire industry through the use of new technology and the change of customer behavior. In the beginning, the company used to send out DVDs for rent via mail. Thus, it essentially was a service that rent DVDs and competed against the physical video rental stores. Nevertheless, next to none of these stores exist anymore, a condition that can be explained by the fact that in 2007 Netflix began its transition to streaming video. The service is based on customer subscription, which allows them to watch any movie or series they want at any time they like. The switch caused an incredibly powerful effect on the video rental and television markets. Any movies or programs any longer required for a person to sit on their couch and watch whatever networks were broadcasting at the moment. Instead, customers could choose precisely what they wanted on platforms like Netflix. The company then proceeded to start creating its own content, including movies and TV shows, which made its position stronger once again. As a result, thousands of physical stores did not survive the transition. Video rental services that previously operated from those stores ceased to exist at all, just like video rental stores. Netflix has also caused severe challenges for television networks, cable companies, and movie developers who have to adapt to the world where any content can be watched at any time, rather than following time schedule. Although Netflix no longer holds the position of the only major streaming service, it is still present as one of the key players of the entertainment industry.

In summary, we conclude that six main notorious disruptors, such as Ford, Kodak, IBM, Southwest Airlines, Apple, and Netflix, demonstrated to companies that new business models, new technologies, or approaches oriented toward customers can disrupt whole industries. The first firm will have a substantial advantage if it manages to recognize the customers' new needs and ask for premium innovations. The consequences of these events were felt by companies and, more importantly, the industries, in which the companies competed, as as a result, the companies either adapted or exited. We will stress that some of them attempted to return and excel in their discipline, albeit the majority of them left for the damage created by the disruptors. We admit that it is very difficult, and can even be very painful, to act in, or adjust to, a disrupted environment. However, we believe that such a period should be considered a period of great opportunities to implement changes and to grow, which is why changes should be accepted and welcome.d It also implies that the businesses that succeed in recognizing the change and disrupting the change will be able to transform the industries with which they interact. We have therefore concluded that the above-mentioned six case studies provide excellent and alternating examples of how disruptions take place, why they are so powerful, and how they have had a whole global impact on the world economy.

Chapter 2 : Emerging Trends in Business Innovation

Technology is one of the key drivers of business model innovation. It defines how companies create, deliver, and capture value. During the last decades, developments in technology have changed entire industries, allowing companies to redesign traditional models and uncover new opportunities for growth. The main concept behind this shift is the versatility of technology, which provides firms with instruments to operate more effectively, reach wider audiences, and create groundbreaking products and services to address customers' needs. One of the key effects of technology on business model innovation is the process digitization and automation.

Cloud computing, artificial intelligence, big data analytics, and robotics process automation, among other tools, allow businesses to make their operations more cost-effective while improving decisions. Cloud computing, for example, allows companies to scale quickly by providing flexible, pay-as-you-go access to computing resources. In this way, they do not need to make large initial investments in physical infrastructure and the management of information technology. Firms can reduce costs and focus on deploying new business solutions and creating value rather than on the technological component. Companies like Amazon Web Services have changed the way businesses look at technology infrastructure, providing even small start-ups with opportunities to compete at a global level, empowered with smart and cost-efficient cloud-based solutions.

Technology has reshaped how businesses operate, streamlining many processes and driving efficiency across the board. With the implementation of better tools and machinery, businesses have been able to produce goods and deliver services more quickly and to higher standards. However, the benefits of technology to businesses are not limited to operational efficiency. Over the past couple of decades, businesses have also been able to find and reach their customers in new and more meaningful ways, enabled by the rise of the power of the internet and the variety of mobile technologies.

Firstly, technology companies have innovated the way they interact with consumers online, with the rise of e-commerce, social media, and mobile apps. The development and adoption of these platforms have facilitated customer engagement and, subsequently, allowed companies to provide more personalized experiences, exactly to the consumers' tastes. Additionally, the data collected from such interactions has provided greater insight into the specifics of consumer behavior, such as frequencies and timings, as well as preferences and online behavior.

Being able to predict and meet those specific consumer needs is the focus of many successful technology companies; for example, Netflix uses data analytics to recommend shows and movies to its users based on their previous views, whereas Amazon provides targeted browsing recommendations to secure purchases. This data also allows refining goods and services for the specific consumers' wants, thereby driving sales and brand loyalty.

There also have been more significant effects on companies and whole industries but the constant evolution of digital technology. Developing, shaping, and maintaining digital ecosystems, such as app stores and online marketplaces, have allowed all varieties of sellers and buyers to transact at their own convenience. Companies like Uber, Airbnb, and Alibaba have been able to grow and sustain their business models, disrupting entire industries. The power of quickly, efficiently, and securely connecting service or goods providers with their immediate customers is difficult to overstate. For example, Uber has upturned the entire taxicab business, by offering a platform for private drivers and commuters, bypassing all regular system checks and company fees. Similarly, Airbnb has revoluzioned the world of hospitality, attracting homeowners who can advertise and rent their rooms and apartments to travelers directly, instead of relying on hotel chains.

On the other hand, technology made the creation of new revenue models possible as well. Subscription services have become very popular lately, as businesses benefit from stable and steady revenue streams. Digital technologies made it possible to sell not a single product but rather a continuous relationship with a customer over an extended period. Spotify and Netflix offer customers access to music or movies, respectively, via monthly subscription fees rather than one-time purchases. This model of operation appeared to be working in virtually any industry, from software-as-a-service Adobe and Salesforce to direct-to-consumer Dollar Shave Club and Blue Apron. Furthermore, business is a prime example of where technology facilitated the development of new revenue models. The internet and social networks make it easy to grow a base of followers and sell a YouTube or Instagram influencer's subscription. Food delivery became more convenient, as drones were introduced to food delivery service. Indoor shrimp farming also became a possible thing due to modern technologies. Wavemaker Labs, a Singapore-based company, developed a suite of products to automate the process, from feeding the shrimp to treating the water. In conclusion, technology has both helped businesses to economize and enabled the creation of new revenue models.

The implication that modern business model innovation is inextricably linked with technology is quite justified. Firstly, technology has made it possible for businesses to access global markets. The development of the Internet and digital platforms has largely removed the entry barriers that prevented enterprises from accessing international customers. E-commerce platforms, digital marketing, and online payment systems now allow even small and medium-sized enterprises to sell their products and services to a wider customer base. The globalization of businesses had a tremendous impact on such sectors as retail, where companies like Alibaba and Shopify have helped millions of entrepreneurs become international manufacturers from scratch. Secondly, technology has enabled business model innovation. In addition to digitizing businesses and enabling new types of interaction with customers, technology has helped companies create platform ecosystems that market other businesses' products or services. All in all, it can be concluded that technology indeed is at the core of modern business model innovation: those who are willing to embrace it will succeed helping their businesses to grow and remain competitive in a continuously changing marketplace.

Current trends such as the sharing economy, subscription services, and platform businesses

Numerous trends in the business environment have been emerging in the modern context that have substantially affected the development of industries and created additional demands from consumers. Among the most impactful trends in modern business, one can outline the sharing economy, subscription business model, and platform business. All three of them are closely related to the development of such a phenomenon as technology and represent innovative ways to generate value. Understanding these trends is vital for organizations that seek to remain competitive in the constantly changing market. The sharing economy can be identified as one of the prominent tendencies of the latest years. In general, the sharing economy can be viewed as an economic model that involves connecting individuals to other people and businesses to exchange or share underused assets or skills for a fee. Innovation in technology has allowed individuals to connect over the web through smartphone apps and websites, and form real economic arrangements to share goods and services, Ian et al., 2019. The trend affected various industries, including such examples as Uber and Lift in transportation, and Airbnb in hospitality.

These firms developed sharing platforms and created an opportunity for individuals with underused assets such as cars or rooms for rent. This opportunity gave rise to one of the most discussed trends in the modern business environment. The sharing economy provided numerous benefits to all parties, as unlike traditional ways of ordering taxi or booking a hotel room, this variant creates an opportunity for people to earn money using their belongings. Allowing people to rent their cars when they are not used instead of requiring them to perform work duties seems especially vital for the transport sector. The capacity to share cars with other drivers on the way to the office and contribute to their expenses with minimal effort provides individuals with significant benefits and makes a profit for the company.

Another significant trend that has been reemerging in recent years is the subscription service business. Subscription-based models imply that customers pay a fee to have continued access to the product or service. It has been a popular method for TV providers, newspapers, and various other companies for many years. However, subscription services have become particularly prevalent in the last decade, as they became a popular business model in industries ranging from media to clothing, and software. This is primarily due to the fact that businesses such as Netflix, Spotify, and Amazon Prime became extremely successful by offering a single, unlimited monthly subscription to all of their content or services. Further, in the software B2B industry, previously one-time purchased programs installed on computers also shifted to subscription services – companies such as Adobe, Microsoft, and NetSuite provide their programs as web services, still charging a subscription fee instead of a one-time payment, and providing the customers with continuous updates and new features. The main draw of subscription services is that they create a continued relationship with the customers, which allows businesses to cater to their needs and potentially reduce churn due to the added overall value of the subscriptions. For customers, subscription services create a more convenient way to consume the products or service, as there is no need for periodic transactions. Most companies providing subscription services also heavily rely on data and analytics, which they use to cater to customers' individual needs and preferences. In comparison to other business, subscription services are able to increase the qualitative and duration aspects of interaction with the customers by constantly engaging with them and offering tailored products or services.

A third significant trend in business, which has been invariably reshaping various markets and industries, is the rise of platform-based businesses. These businesses employ platform business models, where a company creates an ecosystem that unites customers, sellers, various service providers, or other entities. These businesses operate as intermediaries between the two parties, creating the necessary IT infrastructure to allow them to communicate. In comparison to a traditional linear business with a central value chain, platform businesses increase in value by connecting, rather than operating within it. The main source of value for these businesses is the previously mentioned network effect, which states that a service becomes more valuable for each of its user as other users also join the service. An example of this would be Twitter, where the more users sign up to the service, the more people other users can send tweets to.

Platform businesses are among the most successful companies in the world today. Amazon is one of the platforms that sells the most. It is one of the world's largest e-commerce platforms, connecting millions of buyers to sellers from all over the world. On the other hand, Facebook or Instagram is the business model that brings together people and advertisers as a social media platform. Another example is Uber and Airbnb, businesses that transport people or connect people with hosts. In conclusion, these businesses have had a huge impact on traditional markets by being more efficient, larger, and more user-friendly. By connecting parties directly, platforms reduce transaction costs and offer convenience. Moreover, as platforms become more popular due to the increased number of service members, users, they benefit from network effects, becoming more valuable to each member as they grow, and becoming more popular. This has helped to create many platforms in a range of new markets; Etsy has created a market for independent artisans and crafters, for example. Upwork and Fiverr have created work-from-home services, and businesses have access to a pool of global talent that has not been hampered by any business model. The ability to attract many investors by being so large and scalable brings considerable added value to the investors. As a result, businesses and consumers should be aware of the main forces in today's modern business environment: the sharing economy, subscription models, and platforms. This is the best way to provide value to customers in the modern world in 2022.

The rise of digital-first companies and virtual business models

Today's global economy is fundamentally different from the one we knew a decade ago, all because of the rise of digital-first companies and virtual business models. These companies exist from Day 1 with all their focus on digital platforms, products, and services, using technology as a driving force for advancing their business. Unlike traditional companies, which could adopt digital solutions in efforts to keep up with the competition or improve their operations, virtual businesses build their value proposition around digital engagement, a virtual infrastructure, and seamless online experiences. This major shift was made possible by the accelerated pace of technology adoption and improvements as well as the increasing availability of the internet and changing consumer preferences. Digital-first companies are very different from their traditional counterparts in many respects, as their virtual nature means that they require fewer physical assets, thus allowing them to grow quicker and be more agile. These companies also extensively rely on cloud computing, big data, AI, and automation. Virtual businesses can reach customers in any part of the world and systematically collect data about their activities to make informed decisions and personalize their experience. Finally, the companies utilizing virtual business models are able to operate without the need to establish physical presence across many locations somewhere in the country or, in some cases, in the world. Instead, online platforms, social media, and digital marketing enable them to have personal relationships with customers across the globe. This vast area of coverage is especially valuable for e-commerce, fintech, and digital content companies that sell their products across the world yet require minimal physical presence to do so.

In addition, the context in which such companies operate is paving the way for a new and highly innovative way of doing business. Thus, digital-first companies can give customers a level of convenience and individual service that cannot be fully realized by traditional businesses. Namely, companies use data analytics and artificial intelligence to customize their goods and services to the desires of individual customers, offering more personalized products and services. For example, e-commerce platforms can offer consumers the products for which they have viewed the history of views, made earlier purchases and their data on behavior. Digital content providers can offer their customers individual video to watch, depending on the consumer's online viewing. This approach leads to high customer satisfaction with the availability of the necessary and quality goods and services, increased customer loyalty, and the growth of sales.

Virtual business models which have emerged with the rise of digital-first companies have enabled companies to be more flexible. Remote work, virtual collaboration, and geographically distributed teams have become the standard for many digital-first companies. These firms are often built on a virtual workforce that has already allowed them to hire the best employees in the world rather than being limited by the need to work in the company building. Thus, the company does not bear the costs of physical office space and employees' hardware and is free to independently determine the number of fully employed personnel, freelancers, or contractors. This approach to business in a virtual cloud environment has proven especially effective in the software development, digital marketing, and customer service industries.

The COVID-19 pandemic only accelerated the switch to exclusively, or in most part, digital-first companies and virtual business models. Due to the fact that lockdown measures often included restrictions for consumers in returning to physical shops due to the threat of infection, and the rise of popularity in internet shopping, businesses that have shifted to digital chains of supply and purchase have seen an increase in demand and growth. In order to adapt to the increased competition, traditional companies had to either start their own digital chain or switch to being a virtual business. COVID-19 has stress-tested the digital-first companies and showcased their high resilience and further growth in a global economy that was heavily disrupted by the pandemic.

To conclude, the digital-first companies and virtual business models are the future of business, showing the new tendencies in leveraging and creating value. The new rule of business – the employment of digital technology to make business more efficient, scalable, and personal – shows no signs of going back, as having been stress-tested in the conditions of a global pandemic, the digital-first companies continue to demonstrate high growth in demand and relevance.

Examples of companies successfully leveraging these trends

There are a number of companies that have successfully employed digital-first strategies and fully virtual business models, becoming the leaders in their respective industries based on the use of technology and innovation that enabled entirely new ways of creating value. These companies are among the most prominent examples of digital-first thinking leading to disruptive success, changing industries and establishing new standards of customer engagement and operational processes. The most prominent example of such a success is probably Amazon, which started as an online bookstore but quickly became one of the biggest e-commerce platforms in the world.

Ever since its creation, Amazon's approach to the business has been digital-first, focusing on leveraging digital technology to provide customers with the opportunity to purchase goods in a way that is convenient, diverse, and cost-efficient. The company quickly expanded beyond the provision of books and added a wide range of consumer product categories to its options, becoming highly dominant in retail. The use of data analytics and sophisticated recommendation algorithms and the development of one of the most advanced logistics networks in the world allows Amazon to give its customers a highly personalized offering, along with a variety of delivery options, some of which provide next-day delivery as part of the Amazon Prime subscription. The company's focus on digital innovation goes beyond e-commerce, with Amazon Web Services being a prominent digital-first platform for businesses that offers cloud computing services.

Netflix has also been one of the companies that has succeeded in the digital-first world. The platform was originally a DVD rental-by-mail service, but it recognized the advantages of employing a digital-first business model that would allow it to offer streaming services. Moreover, by taking advantage of growing advances in digital streaming and cloud computing, Netflix as an organization transformed itself, becoming a key industry player of the modern era and driving the development of the television and movie industry. Its operations have been accompanied by substantial investments in analytics, enabling the firm to draw on information about users' preferences, as well as the approaches that led to the highest levels of consumption in order to develop original content. Netflix's product, shows like Stranger Things and The Crown, were among those created using the application of its analytics-based model, which was instrumental in its growth. Overall, Netflix's successes are highly indicative of the possibilities associated with employing digital-first business models, and its shows help to ensure its attraction in an ever-growing and competitive market.

Shopify has also become one of the textbook examples of successful digital-first companies. The business developed a platform that enabled its clients to create their digital storefronts, offering a combination of digital tools that made it easier for its users, who are entrepreneurs and firms, to develop an e-commerce platform. The model capitalizes on the increasing interest among both individual entrepreneurs and small businesses in working specifically over the digital medium, enticing their customers to purchase the goods and services created by using Shopify's tools. Moreover, the company's models are based on a subscription, enabling it to rely on a more predictable form of revenue, which is one of the key contributor's to its high profitability and scale potential.

The transportation sector brings the most salient example of a digital-first companies. Indeed, Uber has expanded its operations without developing a 'brick-and-mortar' dimension, transforming mobility without owning a single vehicle. Uber's virtual business model works through an application designed to make potential passengers. Uber collects private drivers willing to offer their services, who are willing to "accept the fares for venturing up to 40 miles". Once the driver and the passenger connect, the system also guides the best route, tracks the driving skills, and charges the fare to the passenger's account safely. Advanced technology allows Uber to update this application in real-time and gather data about supply and demand, the most frequently requested destinations, and so on. This flexibility also enables the company to adapt quickly to market and consumer changes, for example, launches of new apps to improve user experience are regular. Moreover, Uber managed to expand globally within a few years, and the lack of physical infrastructure was a great adventage. Hence, Uber is one of the most famous examples of digital first companies that make us think differently about transportation and work.

However, a similar role in the financial sector should be ascribed to Stripe. Instead of managing a single user, receptors, and payments, the company created a digital platform that allows vendors to receive their dues painlessly and quickly. The company also developed an API that integrates smoothly into e-commerce platforms, making life easier for digital natives. 'Brick-and-mortar' restrictions did not impact Stripe's growth and marketability, making it the most powerful player in the fintech area.

Finally, Zoom is an example of a company perfectly corresponding to the idea of digital-first and virtual business models. Zoom is an online video conferencing tool built on a cloud-based platform. During Covid-19, a vast number of businesses, schools, and households had to shift to virtual communication, and Zoom was one of the easiest, most reliable, and available tools for the purpose. The company's platform allows conducting both regular video calls and webinars and proved to be an optimal way to switch to remote work and other activities for millions of users worldwide. Thanks to being cloud-based, Zoom managed to respond to the rapidly growing demand and scale overnight to fulfill users' needs. Security, reliability, and an extremely user-friendly interface made Zoom the leader in the niche. One can conclude that the increasing importance of digital-first models may help companies of all kinds embrace the change and react immediately to the situation due to the available technological innovations.

These examples prove that digital-first companies and virtual business models can have a considerable disruptive potential, enhance innovation, and achieve rapid growth due to technological approaches. Such companies operate in the fields of e-commerce, content delivery, transport, and financial services, and remote communication. They revolutionize regular business practice, allowing companies to diminish their reliance on in-person interactions and promote the development of excellent technology. Given the increasing importance of digital-first models, more companies are likely to follow this example and impact the modern business landscape.

Chapter 3: The Subscription Economy: Beyond Products, Towards Relationships

Businesses in countless industries have shifted to a subscription-based model, transforming the way customers interact with brands and consume products or services. Instead of selling customers a product or service once, subscription services provide customers with an object they can use or a service they can access in exchange for regular fees. As a result, the dynamic between businesses and customers is constantly changing, redefining the value to which consumers are willing to subscribe. In particular, the concept of a continuous and personalized service is one of the most significant changes. Even after making a purchase, customers now expect businesses to provide services or products that match them over an extended period. Instead of treating a purchase as a one-off event that may not affect a relationship with a given company in the future, subscription models encourage a dynamic relationship that requires the company to engage with customers on a regular basis. For example, businesses must provide regular updates, new content, or enhancements. At the same time, companies must continuously gather feedback on the experience and how it can be improved.

Second, customers are more demanding when it comes to the convenience or flexibility with which they can access a service or product. Subscription services and models have enabled businesses to provide customers exactly what they want, when they want it, thanks to the rise of on-demand content and meal kits, as well as subscription boxes for everyday goods. In this way, customers can set their preferences and receive items right away — they do not have to worry about going to the store themselves or making a conscious effort to obtain an item. Continuing productivity is another straightforward desire. Since customers are now paying regularly, they expect a fair share of constant value from the companies to which they offer their money. For instance, a company may provide exclusive shows or songs to their core subscribers in the case of digital content. On the other hand, in the case of companies that provide physical products that can be palates or aesthetics, they must prove their worth by delivering a consistently high level of product. Ultimately, while a one-time purchase does not have an impact on future interactions, a subscription model necessitates a high degree of customer satisfaction. Customers are free to terminate their subscriptions if they are unhappy and the companies they are doing business with are ultimately responsible for doing what it takes to keep them subscribed.

Benefits and Challenges of Implementing a Subscription Model

1. Why would a company want to enable the subscription model for their goods or services? What are the key benefits of this model?

The subscription model can offer multiple benefits for businesses, but it is also associated with a set of challenges. One of the main benefits is the possibility of having predictable, recurring revenue. Unlike traditional business models, where companies depend on sporadic sales, subscriptions can provide a company with a continuous, relatively stable source of income. This enables better planning on the company's side, as they can allocate resources more effectively and implement long-term growth strategies. Moreover, a subscription model can make a business more appealing for investors, as it implies a more stable and scalable revenue model. Another important benefit of the subscription model is the opportunity to build strong relationships with customers and boost their loyalty. The more often a customer interacts with a company, the more data can be gathered about them, assisting in catering to ever-changing preferences. In addition, characterised by a focus on recurring revenue, subscription businesses can develop better skills and technologies for promoting customer stickiness.

2. Why would a company not want to enable the subscription model for their goods or services? What are the main risks?

Although enabling the subscription model can be associated with multiple benefits, it is also linked with some risks. The first major risk that is associated with adopting the model is the challenge of customer acquisition. Although the idea of having recurring revenue, as well as the possibility of crating customer relationships more effectively, may seem attractive, finding subscribers can be more difficult than executing a single sale. Customers may be more wary of committing to a long-term purchase, especially if they are unfamiliar with the value the product or service would bring to them. Hence, substantial marketing efforts and activities related to explaining the model to the customer may be required. Another risk is the need to ensure the focus on continuous innovation of the product or service. In the subscription model, the company interacts with customers on a continuous basis, rather than a single instance of sale. As a result, there is a continuous expectation to bring value to the customers' lives and prevent them from cancelling the subscription. Finally, even happy customers can cancel the subscription when they consider it too expensive, or believe they do not need it at a particular moment. Thus, this would require a subscription business to develop a solid customer retention strategy, which is not always an easy task. Moreover, even in the case of customers deciding to churn, efforts can be spent on retaining them with flexible plans or other approaches.

Case Studies of Companies like Netflix, Spotify, and Dollar Shave Club

A number of companies successfully utilized subscription-based models to disrupt an industry and become leaders in it. The most prominent examples are Netflix, Spotify, and Dollar Shave Club. Netflix is among the first and strongest disruptors of the subscription-based streaming industry. In the 1990s, the company offered a DVD rental-by-mail service. After revolutionizing the video rental market by developing an online distribution logic and significantly undercutting the competition, Netflix penetrated the streaming market. As digital content became a modern consumer's choice because of its convenience and immediate access, Netflix had an impressive infrastructure of data on customer preferences. Therefore, Netflix creates a highly personalized experience for the viewer by determining what shows they would like based on factors such as content length, summary, and previous viewing experiences. The key to the company's success is in content, especially self-produced series and movies such as Stranger Things and The Crown. These exclusive dishes are highly popular and, combined with a large volume of data, make it difficult for competitors to succeed as strongly in the market. As the number of competitors in the market grows, the importance of exclusive content will increase, and thus, one can confidently state that Netflix will remain on top even after integrating the industry further. Spotify's subscription-based streaming service also greatly affected the music industry. The service's premium subscription, which fits most listeners, offers ad-free listening and higher audio quality and allows users to listen in the offline mode. However, the main feature is a virtually unlimited personalized music listening feature that does not have any actual restrictions in terms of time and only costs $10 per month. The service is one of the most popular in the world, and its method of taking advantage of a product that is not used at its full capacity due to external factors to benefit both the company and consumers was revolutionary. Another example of a company utilizing a subscription service model to disrupt the market that deals in physical goods is Dollar Shave Club. Before the launch of the company, the vast majority of people bought razors like the ones produced by Gillette in the store as their prices were lower. Thus, the company reached market dominance with a strategy that was previously used by other entrepreneurs. With a low-cost subscription service that is easy to sign up for and offers home delivery, Dollar Shave Club has been able to generate a significant amount of income. With a significant marketing campaign conducted mainly through video and social media support and producing a product of the same quality as its competitor's, Dollar Shave Club became a leader overnight. When the value of the company became undeniable, within one month of the analytics company's statement that it was worth $200 million, the company was purchased by Unilever for $1 billion. The case of Dollar Shave Club proves the effectiveness of subscription-based models for disrupting traditional industries.

Key Considerations for Entrepreneurs Interested in Subscription-Based Services

Entrepreneurs who consider establishing a subscription-based service should take into account several important nuances to maximize the success of their business. One of the most critical factors is a proper understanding of the target market. Not all goods and services suit the subscription model, and it is necessary to recognize the market segment that will benefit from its products through a subscription. Entrepreneurs should analyze if their offering solves an ongoing problem or satisfies a continuous need that can make clients bound to the service in the long term. For instance, digital content, frequently used products, such as grooming items, or ongoing services, like software availability, are often suitable for subscriptions. Pricing strategy should also be a priority, as the subscription model presupposes lower upfront costs but requires retaining clients for a more extended period to produce profits. Entrepreneurs should determine the optimal balance between affordability and the value of their product or service, as they need to secure a constant stream of subscribers. They can also opt for multiple pricing plans, such as membership tiers or pay-as-you-go availability, to suit various customer needs and budgets.

Customer experience is another area of concern, as subscription-based businesses profit from multiple interactions with clients. Entrepreneurs should select technology and organizational structure that will allow efficient on boarding, individualized recommendations, and cancellation opportunities. The smoother and more intuitive the process, the more likely is the client to become involved in a long-term relationship, and, conversely, any problems and obstacles prompt immediate churn. Entrepreneurs should also consider retention strategies, as even with the best approach, some portion of the clients will choose to cancel their subscription. Providing regular updates, adding extra services, or engaging clients with loyalty programs and exclusive offerings could help sustain the perceived value of the subscription in the long term. Involving clients in the process, receiving their feedback, and addressing their specific needs will also assist in developing products and services that will be more appreciated by them. However, entrepreneurs should remember that the best way to promote long-term subscriptions is to innovate continuously. In a world increasingly marred with subscription fatigue, when the customers are abandoning the business model as unsustainable, entrepreneurs should always offer fresh and relevant content, products, or services. Whether it is entirely new product lines, additional exclusive features, or an exclusive star-studded experience, entrepreneurs must innovate to keep their subscriptions exciting.

Chapter 4: Platform Businesses and the Network Effect

Platform business is a business model that enables the exchange of value among two or more interdependent groups through a central infrastructure. Such groups are usually producers and consumers, and the firm does not produce the product or service that is being exchanged. The firm creates an ecosystem where different users can interact with each other. In platform businesses, the core component is the platform, allowing users to connect, communicate, and transfer. There are many specific types of business platforms, but the most important feature is that they do not produce products or services but the infrastructure that can be used to create value. Such businesses exclude the process of production and focus solely on creating an infrastructure for other parties to interact with no need to own the exchanged value. Eventually, these businesses scale fast and to much greater extents than conventional companies.

The traditional business model uses the pipeline approach, where value is created and goes down the funnel from one party to the other. As a simple example of a manufacturing company, the process looks like the owner of the factory creates a product that is then transported to the retailer and eventually to the customer to be sold. This demand requires the purchase and control of the maximum amount of resources and assets because the business itself is involved in most stages of creation and selling.

In conclusion, the platform business relies on creating a network or platform as a central foundation for value exchange. Firms then rely on other parties to create value that is exchanged through this platform. Platforms create a set of network rules to follow the exchanged value and sets of rules to ensure trust among participants. The value is then exchanged by pairs of users, different transactions for which platforms can charge fees, offer subscriptions, or serve as advertisement platforms depending on the principles.

Understanding Network Effects and Their Role in Scaling a Platform

Network effects are a crucial aspect of success for platform businesses. The network effect appears when a product or service becomes more valuable as more people use it. In the case of platform businesses, it implies that the greater number of users a platform managed to attract, the more valuable it becomes for all stakeholders. There are two types of network effects: direct and indirect. A direct network effect occurs when the addition of more users increases the value of the system for all existing users. An excellent example is provided by social media platforms, such as Facebook and Instagram. With each additional user, the platform becomes more valuable to all others because the potential size of the network that can be accessed through the platform is larger. The indirect effect of the network is observed when more users join the one side of the platform, making the system more valuable for users of another platform. The example is found in Airbnb, a large set of hosts, attracts and benefits travelers, as the larger available housing base. The increase in travelers, estimated at the same time, can enrich the offer of housing. Similarly, the raising number of riders benefits the drivers who cooperate with Uber. In her turn, the larger number of drivers makes the service more repeatedly for riders to use.

Network effects facilitate the scaling of platform businesses because they create a positive loop: the platform is growing with the addition of new users, they attract other users with their resources. Once a critical mass is achieved, the potential financial gain of people associated with a particular platform becomes too great for it to be abandoned in favor of another, which leads to an exponential growth trajectory. Besides, network effects erect a significant barrier to entry for the competitors. As the platform becomes more entrenched, and the number of participants grows, it is increasingly harder to start a similar platform that would have the same value for the users, making it less probable for newcomers to challenge former platforms. However, the task of creating network effects is not automatic. Companies of platform businesses should manage the delicate balance between two sides of the market, supply of goods and the demand for them. For instance, eBay should attract sellers to provide products that buyers want to buy. If there are too many vendors and not enough buyers on the platform, then the sellers will not see any value in selling their products on the platform. Conversely, if there are too many buyers and too few sellers on the platform, these buyers will not have a product for which they would like to pay. Keeping these two sides of the platform in equilibrium is vital for establishing and maintaining the effects of the network.

Case Studies of Successful Platform Companies Like Airbnb, Uber, and Alibaba

Many platform businesses have successfully employed network effects to disrupt traditional industries and become the dominant players in the global economy. Airbnb, Uber, and Alibaba are good examples of how the business models centered around the value of networks can scale and reshape the markets. Airbnb facilitated the rise of the shared economy concept and introduced a brand new type of company operating in the hospitality sector. Airbnb gave an opportunity for the owners of houses, apartments, or rooms to rent them to travelers. As these travelers increasingly decided to use the platform, hosts received an increasing number of incentives to list their properties. The growing supply of properties only fed the growing demand from the travelers. At the same time, the success was contained in the focus on creating the platform with the high level of trust on both sides, which was guaranteed through creating clubs, insuring the hosts, and implementing the comprehensive review showing. As a result, the demand and supply growth reinforced the company's expansion, and now, Airbnb operates in more than 200 countries, disrupting a traditional and decades-long-or centuries-long-existing business of hotels.

Another platform business that employed network effects to disrupt a traditional market, the market of transportation, this time, is Uber. A substitute to a taxi, Uber is a mobile app that links the drivers and riders. In order to effectively expand in new markets, Uber focused on a continuous acquisition of drivers to ensure that enough supply was available to meet the growing demand form the riders. As the number of drivers increased, the service became more reliable for the riders, which resulted in an increasing use of the platform that was readily available. Uber used a combination of measures to retain its attractiveness, such as the implementation of dynamic pricing, reliance on real-time data, and guarantee of a seamless user experience. Now, Uber operates in more than 900 metropolitan areas all around the globe, disrupting the transportation and taxi industries all over the world.

The most successful platform business in the world, especially in the e-commerce sector, is Alibaba. Alibaba is an online marketplace for buyers and sellers, which was established in 1999 in China. In contrast to Amazon, which is considered to be a hybrid platform employing a combination of a direct sales model and a third-party platform, Alibaba created an ecosystem that linked sellers and buyers without much involvement of the company. The platform is used by both Chinese retailers and international businesses. The success of Alibaba was dependent on an ability to create a vast ecosystem, which included not only the e-commerce but also payment solutions, logistics, and cloud computing, effectively transforming the business for businesses that were willing to sell the products. The network effects allowed Alibaba to outrun many other businesses, with hundreds of millions of active users and billions of transactions running through the systems of the company.

Practical Steps for Building and Growing a Platform Business

Creating and growing a platform business requires proper planning, focusing on user experience, and the ability to scale both sides of the ecosystem. Given that information, below are simple steps for anyone planning to develop and establish a platform business.

Simple Steps to Build the Platform Business

1. Start by creating a real-value proposition

This step is important in starting any business, and platform business is not an exception. It is important to create a platform that facilitates producers' and consumers' transactions in meaningful ways. Before formation and starting the platform design, it is important to determine the value side that the platform will provide. For example, Uber offered a fast and convenient way to call cabs. Before Uber, the fastest way to get a cab was by using a phone call. The worth of Airbnb was cheap and butchered lodging. In conclusion, it is important to focus and serve both of the sides by understanding their requirements for creating a service that will attract them.

2. Building trust and reducing friction

The most significant challenge for a platform business is creating and promoting trust. On an e-commerce-supervised platform, this trust is maintained between sellers and buyers. As for lodging platforms, the trust is built and maintained between hosts and their guests. Therefore, it is important to work on ways of reducing the friction and building a trust chain. This can be achieved by employing mechanisms like customer reviews, ratings, and verification. Secure payment methods should be equally employed, and customer service offered.

3. Investment in user experience and technology

One of the most successes and failure deciding factors of a platform business is the ability to focus on the user experience. Generally, most platforms that consider technology to promote the user experience are likely to succeed. This would mean creating a simple and intuitive platform that can be used on multiple users' devices. The best potential a platform business can achieve is through scalable, low-latency and high-degree secure data infrastructure. Building a latency-free and scalable platform is possible through the use of optimal machine learning and data analytics.

4. Attract critical mass on both sides of the platform: A typical condition for the success of a platform is the achievement of a critical mass of users on the supply side and demand side. As a result, entrepreneurs need to attract enough producers to meet consumers' needs and vice versa. With this in mind, they can work on package offerings, such as reducing fees for the participants or offering them a bonus. The balance between supply and demand is crucial to lay the groundwork for implementing this principle and developing network effects since consumers or producers on one side of the platform are more likely to join when there is already a sufficient number on the other side.

5. Use data to improve and grow the platform: Considerations based on empirical data and user information are valuable for platform businesses. Entrepreneurs can make mining this

information a priority and analyze the derived data to learn how they can enhance their platform and stimulate its growth. For example, they can learn more about users' needs, wants, and experiences, and adjust the way their platforms work to serve their interests. To achieve these goals, they need to invest in collecting and analyzing the data and devising ways to act on their findings that are integrated into their platforms through feedback loops.

6. Expand geographically or into other markets: If a platform proves to be successful in one market, entrepreneurs may consider expanding in other areas either geographically or vertically. For instance, Uber started as a ride-sharing platform and later expanded its offerings, such as a food delivery service, with UberEats. Similarly, Airbnb initially worked as a vacation rental provider and later increased its range to experiences and other travel-related services. As a result, entrepreneurs can increase their platforms' user base, revenue, and the resulting market power.

Chapter 5: The Sharing Economy and Access over Ownership

The phenomenon of the sharing economy has contributed to a significant shift in people's attitudes toward ownership. Previously, in the traditional economy, ownership of various items played an essential role for a person. It allowed one to demonstrate wealth, ensure security, and make a contribution to economic development. Individuals and corporations invested in real estate, vehicles, equipment, and other assets because the latter were viewed as important for creating long-lasting value. In contrast, the sharing economy requires people and companies to own fewer items. They can be shared and used as required instead of purchased. The phenomenon is facilitated by technology apps that provide comprehensive analytics. The overall impact of the sharing economy is a more efficient acquisition process and fewer assets that need to be owned. When using the logic of the sharing economy, one should also consider that the phenomenon presupposes people's greater importance as resource owners. As a result, people are allowed to share underused assets.

The creation of the phenomenon in question was conditioned by the widespread use of technology. Sharing was facilitated by online platforms where people can communicate directly with each other and identify the value of the resource. Users have open access to instruments, such as apps and websites, where they can choose from a wide range of resources. Online resources also provide real-time information. In this way, the sharing economy is made possible because people use these resources to assist other users by providing them with timely information. In the past, the availability of such resources was limited, and rental agencies, restaurants, and shops acted as intermediaries instead of their owners. This means sharing was impossible. In addition, the possibilities of the sharing economy are based on the maximum utilization of existing resources. For example, a person may not need a car, house, or an otherwise used item every day. Instead of owning the item outright, they can rent one they need today and save resources for tomorrow. Overall, the sharing economy helps people establish more sustainable consumption models, reduce expenditures, and minimize waste.

More importantly, however, the phenomenonulates a new approach to ownership, which implies that an asset is used for a certain period instead of the duration of its service. One of the main reasons customers follow this pattern is the convenience of use and lack of extra effort required to own the item. It is important that as more and more people follow this approach, industries begin to change their ideas. Therefore, in the nearest future, a new model may arise when ownership will no longer be a priority.

The Impact on Industries Like Transportation, Real Estate, and Goods Rental

The sphere of sharing economy has significantly affected the existence of several industries, including transportation, real estate, and goods rental. In each sector, considerable disruption has occurred as new business models challenge the more traditional ways to deliver value to end-users. Firstly, in terms of transportation, the idea of such companies as Uber, Lift, and Zipcar has changed the approaches to getting from one place to another. In the circumstance of the traditional managing and owning a car, many people can nowadays benefit from the availability of automobiles that can be delivered at their request depending on the urgency of their need. As a result, fewer people, especially in urban areas, can own a car since they can take advantage of a diversified service that can bring up a vehicle to them when necessary. Convenience in this context is evident, as fewer cars on the roads contribute to fewer greenhouse gas emissions and gas usage. Moreover, it is evident that via one's ability to get where they want via the app, new standards of convenience for other types of more traditional taxi services have been set. Not adapting to these changes requires such service providers to either rapidly change their business models and leverage the use of applications or suffer the challenges of poor adaptability.

The real estate scenario has also been affected by the changes as a result of the introduction of the idea of the sharing economy where such companies as Airbnb and WeWork benefit from the lower vulnerability of stayers and renters in terms of making decisions on where to stop or rent for a period. Airbnb is perhaps the most well-developed platform of this type where most listings either equal or exceed the traditional hotels in terms of travelers' demands. WeWork is another type of Airbnb, hosting a greater number of startups and new companies on their premises in their pursuit of providing collaborative space for business owners and entrepreneurs. These conditions are typical of commercial real estate residents who obtain the perks of not needing to rent a space for a long time and do not invest in any co-working areas. Goods rental is also a modified sector as a consequence of the idea of the sharing economy. Platforms like Rent the Runway provide the ability for clients to hire luxurious items instead of buying them, with clothes produced mainly for app consumers. Here this platform provides a highly convenient experience for end-users who want to rent clothes, tools, and other items on a temporary basis rather than pay for a high upfront price for the possession of a particular item. In general, the sharing economy concept imposes a higher value upon access, rather than ownership.

Case Studies of Companies Like Zipcar, Rent the Runway, and We Work

Several companies have built their business on the principles of the sharing economy. Moreover, many of such organizations have disrupted the landscapes of their industries, changing them permanently. Zipcar, Rent the Runway, and WeWork are examples of such projects that presented novel values to their users and attracted many participants. Zipcar, for instance, was among the first to allow individuals to use cars without owning them. Rent the Runway lets users rent designer clothes instead of buying them. WeWork offers shared workspaces for various companies. Each of these examples of sharing economy businesses demonstrates how such services can flourish by employing innovative approaches to traditional services and respond to consumers' unmet needs.

Zipcar was one of the first to introduce the idea of sharing cars to the general public. Using the developed app, consumers can easily find available vehicles in their cities, pick them up from the streets, and return them afterward. The primary advantage of Zipcar is users can employ cars without buying them and avoid high expenses and the necessity to live near large parking. However, it allows people to reduce their burden while owning cars and, possibly, the number of purchased vehicles. Instead, cars are available, as if they belong to the users themselves. Here, two main benefits can be identified regarding ownership and environmental needs.

Rent the Runway is another telling example of effectively employing concepts of sharing economy. Launched in 2009, the platform now offers thousands of designer and everyday clothes from hundreds of prestigious brands. The sharing feature is that users do not buy these clothes but rent them for some time and then return. This approach is very beneficial for Rent the Runway clients due to two main reasons. New clothing changes every week and allows people to be more sustainable while never having to worry about fashion trends.

WeWork was founded in 2010 and presented people, mostly owners of small businesses and startups, with shared rental office spaces, including modern building technologies, efficient use of workspace, and a vast online archive. At the moment, the company has 527 locations in 111 cities worldwide. People and companies can rent work desks or premises for their organizations. The primary advantage of WeWork is a lack of binding. Greater companies rent workplaces in WeWork when it is convenient for them, and new small firms can go to new places to open new offices. Ways of cooperation and work are arranged by WeWork to create a spirit and space for client companies' interaction. The main benefits are relevant for people whose working environment often changes or those who run small ones that have a long-term vision to expand. Noticeably, each of the bambooish examples effectively employed technological innovations to create new values for their clients.

Strategies for Entering and Succeeding in the Sharing Economy

The sharing economy has attracted a significant amount of interest, as many consumers search for more sustainable, affordable, and, in some cases, ethical ways to acquire access to goods and services. This trend promotes the need for more alternatives, which creates an opportunity for entrepreneurs. However, launching a platform for shared access to goods or services is not sufficient for success.

In order to outperform competitors, reduce risks, and establish a viable business in the sharing economy, companies should benefit from existing assets, build consumer trust, develop a scalable and user-friendly platform, and consider any additional features that can be offered.

The high saturation of the sharing economy demands for viewing underutilized assets and resources, which can be shared or rented. Cars, homes, office spaces, and luxury clothing can all be successful examples, as they are expensive to own, seldom used, or both. Throughout all industries, entrepreneurs should look at what they already have access to and then think about how other customers will want to have access to something in a less expensive or more sustainable way. EZ Texting's assets, processes, and user base could have been implemented to propose an affordable alternative for companies to promote their texting services through direct access to 180,000 clients.

Moreover, all platforms in the sharing economy are peer-to-peer, which makes it crucial to establish a concept of trust and security. Trust can be built around the opportunity to receive reviews, customers' ratings, and people's verification, in addition to the use of side features, such as insurance or seal of approval. All platforms in the sharing economy aim to establish a sense of security and transparency, and many of them possess relatively low penalties for failure in order not to waste assets. For example, UKCoworking provided a platform focusing on paid access to desks and co-working spaces in people's homes and also offered a guarantee for hosts in the case of potential damage.

Finally, it is essential to develop a platform that is scalable and easy to use. RS1 has invested in modern technology, including mobile applications. Data analysis, data storage, and database processing include platforms and payment systems, but it is completely customized because many systems do not work offline. Having a scalable platform, for example, can invest in steady growth while ensuring that the quality of the service will still be consistent with the needs of a wider audience. It is kept user-oriented. All features improve the performance of the shared platform.

In order to complement an already profitable asset, develop the trust concept, the scale, and the integration of relevant features, entrepreneurs should also consider their existing resources. It is crucial to develop the capacity of the existing resource and its related network. On the platform, they will be able to develop various business deals, and when building the company, how to acquire and expand their presence into applicable brands are other subjects for consideration. References

Chapter 6: Social Enterprise and the Triple Bottom Line

Social enterprises are businesses who aim to generate both financial profit and social or environmental impact. They attempt to address society's problems through creative solutions, using a market-based approach to drive systemic change. While regular businesses operate with single-minded focus on maximizing shareholder value, these purpose-driven businesses develop a new form of capitalism, which allows for not only profit motive, but also emphasis on their impact on people and the planet. Therefore, social enterprises occupy a unique niche between for-profit and non-profit business, creating sustainable solutions for the world's pressing issues by combining their attributes. Their appeal lies in the novel business opportunities they create. Purpose-driven business models provide solutions to social and environmental problems that can be effectively scaled and maintained in a sustainable way. Furthermore, these business models challenge traditional approaches to capitalism and enrich the concept by incorporating long-term perspective. Such initiatives are centered around creating business value for both the shareholders and all other stakeholders or even society as a whole. Social enterprises create shared value by having a social mission at the very core of their operations. This drives their performance and innovation as it makes business success dependent on the well-being of society and the environment. In an age where, especially among millennials and members of Generation Z, the consumer trend points towards spending money on products and services that align with personal values and ethics, purpose-driven business models are particularly relevant as they appeal to value-driven purchases. People want to buy from, work for and invest in businesses that do good in the world. Therefore, they can attract non-traditional customers, workers and impact investors, gaining a competitive edge.

The Concept of the Triple Bottom Line: People, Planet, and Profit

The idea of the triple bottom line is rooted deeply in the principles of social enterprises. According to the concept developed by John Elkington in the 1990s, the triple bottom line is a business approach that evaluates the performance of a company in three key dimensions: people, planet, and profit. In social enterprises, this notion becomes even more significant, as it allows developing a business model that generates economic value and improves communities' well-being by delivering higher-quality products or services. The concept of the triple bottom line allows moving focus from financial statements to include social and environmental assessments, thus making companies accountable for their impact on a wider range of stakeholders.

The first "P" in the triple bottom line model stands for people, which refers to the social aspect of doing business. In social enterprises, people rely on the principles of fairness and justice in the treatment of employees, stakeholders, and communities. In other words, a social enterprise should care about all people that might be affected by its performance. This dimension presupposed creating jobs for marginalized or disempowered people, ensuring safe working conditions, and supporting local economic development. In a word, the people component in the triple bottom line approach evaluates the impact a company has on citizens and their communities.

The second key aspect of the triple bottom line approach is related to the planet, or the environmental dimension. For social enterprises, that implies environmentally-oriented enterprises, the aspect of the planet refers to eco-conscious products or services. Social enterprises try to enhance their environmental performance by implementing recycling output, using recyclable materials, or synthesizing biodegradable products. In such a way, the planet aspect of the triple bottom model refers to a social enterprise, that ensures that all the processes do not harm the environment.

Finally, the third letter in the model is the profit aspect. In social enterprises, even though making a profit is a critical point, investors use their profits not as the ultimate goal of the business, but as a resource or an instrumental goal. In other words, maximizing profits is just a means of ensuring the further development of the enterprise and the accomplishment of social or environmental mission. Thus, the triple bottom approach opens up a way for a people- and planet-friendly model of doing business.

Case Studies of Companies Like TOMS Shoes, Warby Parker, and Patagonia

There are several examples of companies where the theory of triple bottom line has been successfully applied. These examples demonstrate that having both a social and environmental mission is possible and, in a way, also advantageous for the core of the business. Three examples are Toms Shoes, Warby Parker, and Patagonia.

Toms Shoes is an excellent example of an idea of "one for one" being taken to a new level when shoes were the need taken into consideration. For each pair of shoes that is sold by Toms, another one is given to a child in need. This has already enabled thousands of children to have a new pair of shoes and, therefore, lead a little bit of a better life. Having started with shoes, Toms expanded its social areas and now also works in providing eyeglasses, water, and supporting safe birth programs around the world. The additional benefit from Toms is the fact that the company does not just work for the good, but also sells its product. This way, it also acquires customer loyalty and provides the customers with an opportunity to help those in need by just making a purchase.

Another example is Warby Parker, an internet eyewear shop that sells relatively cheap and quality-heavy glasses. Similarly to Toms, Warby Parker also sells they eyewear according to the one-for-one model where pairs of glasses bought by customers are matched with pairs forwarded to people that are in need of them. This had made the business even more attractive to the millennial that might not be very big on buying something other than food, clothes, or a place to live and expect something in return that would match the much-needed benefit they get from a new pair of glasses with an opportunity to present someone else with the same benefit.

Finally, a third example is Patagonia, a very well-known and already established in terms of business company that was founded with a social and environmental mission in mind. It supports environmental funds to which the company donates 1% of its sales, supports fair trade, and its customers, whenever they decide against buying another thing, are suggested by the company itself to think whether they could repair the old instead. In this way, Patagonia products might not be always sold as much as they would be if consumers would buy new stuff and throw the old ones away, but the company has attracted a considerable bunch of environmentally-conscious people who will always opt for the environmentally-friendly Patagonia product, and there are enough of them on this planet to keep the company in a healthy financial state.

How Entrepreneurs Can Align Profit with Purpose and Scale Impact

If social entrepreneurs want to create purpose-driven businesses, the profit should be in line with the impact. On the one hand, environmental and social enterprises cannot solve the issue if they fail to produce revenue, which means that if they want to be successful, they should also have a positive effect on the environment. Hence, aligning profit with impact should be done from the very start of the enterprise, as those who base their efforts on charity or rely solely on donations are generally unlikely to succeed in achieving their mission.

The first step for an entrepreneur is to carefully define their mission and make it an integral part of their business reality. If an entrepreneur might seek to address a social or environmental issue they perceive as important, their business model should be focused on making a difference in that particular context. For instance, if a company is addressing the issue of plastic waste, it might base its production on sustainable materials, design products that can last for multiple applications or parts of which can be recycled, and donate money to organizations working on the issue. In many cases, the mission becomes the starting point and the core of the business, around which all other aspects are organized.

Social entrepreneurs should also measure and track the impact of their brand. Social enterprises should be able to prove the beneficial effect they have on people and the environment and provide hard data on the number of people employed and other similar parameters. As statistics prove that the idea of using the revenues of social enterprises for the purpose of investment in the development of the organization is certainly a good idea, having information on the impact might also be slightly more accurate. These data will also help in finding partnerships to scale the enterprise in the desired fashion. Additional data and performance improvement via quality metrics will help in expanding impact. Creating networks is another means to expand the impact of the enterprise, as creating and fostering partnerships with other non-profit organizations in the sector or even government organizations will contribute to the scalability of social entrepreneurship. Accounting for scaling via technology is also an important part of the approach to the alignment of profit and impact.

Many software solutions can be used in order to effectively measure the impact of a social enterprise in a particular sector. For many social enterprises, it is also possible to improve performance by using data gathered via digital means and improve operations for better efficiency. For instance, social entrepreneurs can consider launching an online store and leveraging such services as cross-selling. They should also ensure quality improvement and get reliable performance data for this. Creating a business model for social entrepreneurship should also account for reduction of labor, automation, and even introduction of other enterprises in the sector to spread the load.

Environment socially conscious entrepreneurs should also consider opting for Eco-friendly materials and make the entire business Eco-friendly. Creating a sustainable business venture is also key to long-term success. Combining these measures into a holistic strategy will ensure a long-term alignment of profit and impact.

Entrepreneurs that want to be successful should try to make sure that their profits are in line with their impact on people and the environment if they want to build purpose-driven business ventures. It is not only necessary but also possible, and it is a great way to make a lasting difference in the world.

Chapter 7: On-Demand Services and the Convenience Economy

Significant improvements witnessed in technology have revolutionized the ways people interact with businesses and the manner in which goods and services are accessed. The concept of the on-demand economy has largely been facilitated by smartphone applications and real-time data analytics. They make it possible for consumers to request various products or services through a single touch of their devices. The simplicity and speed of on-demand platforms are among the fundamental factors that have redefined overall customer service provision. A range of vital customer expectations, including immediacy, convenience, and accessibility, is now central to the modern business environment. Notably, the primary force driving this ordering revolution is impatience or the need for instant gratification. For instance, people do not want to wait for days to receive their orders or employ elaborate processes in the selection of service providers. Thus, on-demand services such as those provided by Instacart, TaskRabbit, or Postmates are becoming increasingly popular among a modern and impatient audience.

The changes in customer behavior are also associated with several important lifestyle changes. Specifically, the growing gig economy, busy lives of urban dwellers, and a rising number of dual-income households have created a situation in which people are willing to pay for convenience. The younger generation, including millennial and Gen Z, also value social networking and experiences more than property ownership. As a result, they tend to follow the long-standing needs philosophy, fearing staying in places devoid of planned and scheduled activity for fear of missing out. Finally, the earlier days have witnessed a complete triumph of mobile devices as the main channel for daily job performance, shopping, and entertainment. Consequently, customers implementing such behavior patterns require that businesses always meet their immediate needs wherever they are. This situation facilitates the on-demand service growth across a vast number of industries.

Opportunities and Challenges in Providing On-Demand Services

Although the on-demand economy provides businesses with numerous opportunities, it raises a number of challenges as well. The primary opportunity is related to the fact that more and more customers are willing to pay for convenience, as this allows consumers to save time.

While they certainly rush to work or home, businesses can either prepare their orders in advance or deliver them to customers before the rival companies will manage to do the same. The model uncovers the other source of profit for businesses because they can either derive added value from existing assets or launch scalable online platforms. The businesses can also change traditional industries by finding faster and more convenient alternatives. In industries like food delivery, taxi services, or home repair, these on-demand companies have the advantage of eliminating the wait for a taxi or an ordered menu, not having the required service or failing to record a timely audit.

Meanwhile, on-demand models offer flexibility and facilitate the optimization of business logistics, allowing companies to monetize their activities and rapidly expand. These cannot but bring about several challenges, particularly because there is always a danger of not being able to meet customer needs as quickly as promised.

All companies that provide services on demand must invest in the company's logistics and ensure the impeccable organization of the entire production and circulation process. The service providers have to constantly monitor all POS machines and prepare them for the often urgent work. As for consumers, the logistics company will need an efficient delivery service, a real-time tracking system, and ideally the biggest network and number of vehicles or delivery personnel. Otherwise, according to two studies in 2019, every sixth user of on-demand delivery services is not satisfied with the service.

Another major challenge is dealing with consumer demand for an on-demand economy more accurately than the companies that decided to ignore the phenomenon. The times when the biggest spikes in demand will be observed, like holidays or special discount offers, are known. If a company fails to make significant expansions, all of its service consumers will quickly move to competitors, and it will be almost impossible to return them.

There are also challenges related to different controls and regulations that need to be taken into account in the context of an on-demand economy. They include worker classification, minimum wage amounts, sick leave, social insurance or consumer/rights protection, as well as individual municipality and professional licensing conditions, which depend on companies and activity sectors. Therefore, all current companies taking part in the on-demand economy need to consider whether they can create a sustainable, up-and-coming business model and test it under current law.

Case Studies of Companies Like Instacart, TaskRabbit, and Postmates

There are several companies which have discovered the potential of a range of on-demand services and used them to change different domains and set up new standards of convenience. Some of the most vivid examples are Instacart, TaskRabbit, and Postmates, which have utilized the benefits of an on-demand model and delivered value to their customers as a result, Also, they have found the right combination of products, delivery features, user-friendly interfaces, and have been able to establish a new type of scalable business for their success and growth. Instacart is one more example of the on-demand economy to receive popularity and success in the industry. It is one of the quickest growing platforms used for grocery shopping and delivery This service may be positioned as a convenient one allowing the customers to receive an order from the nearby store in a few hours. One of the reasons for the company's success is the ability to meet the growing demands for convenience. With the help of Instacart, the customers have access to a wide range of products from the major grocery store chains and do not need to leave their homes. Another example is TaskRabbit, which industry is the professional business. People require services in some types of repair services, cleaning services, furniture, or other equipment assembly services. It is often the case that people do not have time, knowledge, or desire to solve some issues. TaskRabbit is a kind of service that allows people to hire temporary workers to come and solve their problems. In my opinion, this company is popular due to its flexibility, which enables the customers to call and order some specialists at a moment's notice and with very reasonable costs. The popularity of services is also easy to understand if a user pays attention to its user-intuitive interface, which helps the customers to find the employees list, read the feedback, and hire someone to complete a task within a few minutes. Finally, Postmates is one more example of the on-demand economy to have been getting more popular recently. This company has established its services across the country to deliver on-demand restaurant, grocery, and retail food delivery. The popularity of the service can be explained through the use of a range of advantages included the fastest serving options compared to similar services, whenever the customers want. The company has become very popular because of its crowd sourcing delivery model, which employs a range of drivers to deliver food as quickly as possible. Also, it has excelled in the use of technology, including the use of its own software to analyze data and deliver the orders as soon as possible.

Essential Elements for Success in the Convenience Economy

To be successful in the convenience economy, businesses need to ensure that several factors are in place. First, is the emphasis on a seamless experience for the customers. The on-demand delivery company should ensure that the platform built for the use of customers is user-friendly and convenient. People who use on-demand services do it due to the convenience; if there is any friction, it can prompt the users to leave. Therefore, the companies should streamline their platforms and develop them in such a way that the users can access the required services with one click. This should also facilitate on-the-go services because the users usually order utilities when they need them and expect them to be delivered on the spot. To ensure this, the logistics and operations of the company should be efficient. Automation can help with forecasting demand based on the data acquired and organizing inventory. The system can then create the most efficient routes for the delivery of the services along with the optimization of the workers and services. Another factor is to ensure that the workers are reliable and try to prevent churn. They are the ones who will deliver the services to the customers and need to have a good relationship with the company if it wants to scale. In addition, businesses are critical to trust and safety regulation and needs to guarantee the qualification of their workers and their identity. Safety is a bigger matter if the company is involved with personal services in the private homes of people.

Worker engagement and fostering a reliable relationship are also ways to drive sales and market the company. Lastly, the important factor to maintain in mind, is scalability. The on-demand services should be able to grow in size and new markets while not compromising its efficiency. Shifting business models and issues on demand can also play a significant role in business development. It will allow the company to be at the front of the innovative processes to ensure that they are ahead of the competition. In such a way, businesses can ensure the success of their on-demand companies by observing these main factors that can drive the success in the convenience delivery market.

Chapter 8: Artificial Intelligence and Data-Driven Business Models

Over the past decade, artificial intelligence has become one of the leading drivers of business innovation, transforming industries by automating processes, facilitating decision-making, and improving customer experience. This term refers to the simulation of human intelligence in machines that are programmed to think and learn, including but not limited to machine learning, natural language processing, and computer vision. AI has also become a powerful tool in the business world, as its capacity to analyze data, detect patterns, and predict outcomes is helping companies get an edge over the competition. The role of AI in business innovation is not confined to automation; it opens new horizons for problem-solving, new product development, and consumer service. This paper argues that AI is an indispensable tool of business innovation due to its capacity to process vast amounts of data and learn from it in ways that were impossible before.

AI's most significant function in the context of business innovation is real-time analysis. Systems based on this technology can process data at a speed that was hitherto impossible in multiple sectors, such as finance, healthcare, retail, and manufacturing. In finance, they can be used for detecting fraudulent transactions as they occur, whereas in the healthcare sector, AI is capable of diagnosing diseases more accurately than humans through the analysis of electronics medical records and imaging data. The importance of AI in data processing capabilities stems from the large sizes of datasets that it is capable of analyzing. Furthermore, when AI is used in this function, it can automatically detect patterns and learn from them, using past data to predict future trends based on a vast pool of examples that human experts would have no time to analyze. This, in turn, generates actionable insights that can drive innovation – for instance, improved efficiency in the prioritization of loan applications – and improve previously bureaucratic procedures.

The business innovation potential of AI is also high in the context of customer service. Its capacity for the analysis of large amounts of data and the detection of patterns can be used in the retail sector for improving consumer service: unlike salespeople, the technology will never fail to recommend an item a customer likes but does not know about. Furthermore, AI has already reformed call centers and other means of communication with customers by transforming voicemails into conversational tools that process information, understand customer needs as callers present them, and synchronously generate pre-programmed answers.

Since it is not limited to any particular area of applicaton and can process data at a rate that is impossible for humans, artificial intelligence is one of the most indispensable tools for business innovation. Any sector has ways in which it can benefit from the analysis of large amounts of information and the generation of actionable insights such as those enabled by AI. Furthermore, with the ever-growing experience in using artificial intelligence, the potential innovation opportunities grow. From the use of driverless cars to the application of predictive maintenance systems, this technology will permit businesses to refine existing methods of operation even further. As such, it is clear that any business complacent enough to not invest in this technology will quickly become obsolete in an increasingly competitive environment.

How Data-Driven Decisions Can Create Competitive Advantages

Data is one of the most valuable assets for businesses today, and AI-powered analytics is a way to use this data for a competitive advantage. Data-driven decisions refer to those made based on the insights obtained from the analysis of available information. AI is good at making meaning of arguably complex data sets leading to more informed decision-making. Such solution is valuable since business benefits largely from reducing uncertainty and risk by predicting the future performance of the company. In the past, some decisions were made on a whim, rather than based on informed knowledge. With AI, companies can analyze previous performance and emerging trends to predict both the future performance and what could be the emerging business opportunities. For example, retailers can have a more accurate view than ever before of what may sell and what is likely to stay on the shelves. AI systems can predict consumer demand leading to a more efficient production process and, ultimately, cost savings.

Furthermore, with AI, companies can offer more personalized services and products than they could ever be able to do in the past. By analyzing a customer's purchase behavior, purchase history, and the preferences of similar customers, AI can help companies understand what exactly the customers might look for. Netflix and Spotify are great examples of subscription businesses using AI to manage their wares. Their recommendation engines go to very fine details to recommend content the users will love. In finance, AI can detect trends much more quickly than the humans do. Some hedge funds now buy AI systems that can read and track news stories. They use this information to make trades before other people can react, that is, before the information becomes public knowledge.

In addition, AI can help to make new business from insights or patterns that some humans would not notice. For example, AI systems can identify that people will buy certain products for their face only if they are also likely to buy a special type of cream to make their appearance more attractive. Thanks to AI, companies can sell the cream alongside these products.

Case Studies of Companies Like Amazon, Google, and IBM Watson

Many companies have already used AI to transform their business models and get a competitive advantage. The good examples of AI-driven organization include such leading corporations as Amazon, Google, and IBM Watson. Probably the most famous application of AI in commerce is the recommendation system developed by Amazon. The online store offers personalized product suggestions based on searching requests, prices, browsing history, and other customers' recorded data. Accordingly, such a shopping experience makes the decision-making process more rational and highlights one's additional demands, increasing the probability of shopping other goods. In addition, the program allowed to significantly optimize the supply chain, starting from demand forecasting to warehouse management, and eliminated the issue of overstocking or overselling of goods. Subsequently, Amazon applied AI to launch its virtual assistant, Alexa and create a new company-consumer interface. The introduction of invaluable and convenient services facilitated the relationship between firm and customers and guaranteed long-lasting trust and devotion to Amazon from its consumers.

Another case of big business utilizing AI is Google with its prominent search engine activities. Indeed, the increasingly popular world's advanced searching system responds to billions of daily requests, providing people with necessary information. In fact, an efficient and sufficient outcome would be impossible without an AI-based controlling system. Furthermore, the company's innovative actions in the field produced multiple implications for research and further development. The obvious example would be Google Assistant, which was created in 2016 to perform numerous tasks for its users, including search and schedule planning. Unfortunately, robotic driving made its first appearance 7 years ago in 2013, Google's autonomous driving system, Waymo utilizes AI for making real-time decisions on the roads. In addition, the corporation succeeded in employing AI in various fields, such as natural language, computer vision, and even administration. Finally, the case of IBM Watson revealed a perfect example of AI is applied to enterprise solutions. Indeed, the programs allow doctors to diagnose patients by comparing their symptoms with existing medical conditions. Moreover, uncountable amounts of information, including all medical literature, enable AI application software to choose the best response, based on the probability of its correctness. In addition, thanks to AI implementation, financial companies can analyze further market tendencies and make profitable predictions. Hence, these examples prove that the case of leading AI corporations integrating AI in their business model helps to get ahead of the competitors and achieve long-lasting success.

Key Strategies for Integrating AI into Business Models Effectively

For businesses, there are several strategies to implement since AI represents a revolutionary technology that has already transformed multiple spheres of human activity. These approaches may be characterized by a set of stages that have been identified in the article "5 Strategies for AI Success". These stages or steps are important for businesses in order for them to experience the benefits of the technology and change their operations. These steps may be summarized in the following way.

As AI can improve several aspects, the first crucial element is to identify the main areas in which the new technology can be applied. In a business, for example, the new system can be integrated into such processes as customer service where chatbots may be used, supply chain management, marketing to provide personalized marketing services, and so on. Moreover, it should be noted that the procedures must be identified on the basis of the relations to the data used, availability of potential human errors or automation, and the use of repetitive tasks.

Since AI systems require specific technologies, businesses will have to make investments in order to establish these processes and machines. Investments may include purchasing hardware and software, but the key element is to identify the pipe procedures and establish these. However, it is even important for businesses to ensure that there will be enough data. Apart from establishing IT infrastructure and signing contracts, it is important to hire relevant professionals. In such a way, the systems will be integrated into the ones and be effectively maintained.

Moreover, enough data must be available, so there should be clear policies and procedures in order to in order to ensure that it is always correct. In such a way, the last stage is to ensure that one has a relevant system, and it is functioning. However, it should be noted that the systems must be divided into small ones in order to build the new models accordingly. In addition, all of them may be regarded to pilot and further improved.

Chapter 9: Blockchain and Decentralized Business Models

Blockchain technology is no doubt one of the most revolutionary technological advancements noticed in the 21st century's business world. To better understand the true meaning of this development, one should keep in mind that its basic principles are the creation of a ledger that is decentralized and distributed across thousands of computing devices. In other words, there is no single record of transactions or ownership of assets or credits, but rather multiple copies of such a record. To change the information stored, one would need to go through all devices where this particular record is stored in a simultaneously synchronized manner, which is practically impossible to achieve.

The primary purpose served by blockchain is, as a result, the creation of trust without the need for an intermediary. Verification of transactions in traditional databases always requires the approval of a central authority. Blockchain, on the other hand, uses a large number of participants in the system, typically called nodes, to verify and approve transactions according to some mechanism of reaching consensus that aims to establish a general record of storage. This latter form of database is most strongly associated with cryptocurrencies and especially with Bitcoin, whose creator and developer, in fact, created this system first. However, the benefits of such a record keeping system are not limited to financial resources, and in fact, this technology is actively used in all kinds of databases such as logistics, healthcare, real estate, and supply chain management.

The reason for the interest in this technology is different for the various businesses. For some, it is the increased transparency that is particularly highly valued. Every transaction in a blockchain system is visible to all participants, which makes it much easier to track the flow of goods, money, or any other types of value resources. This feature, for example, is an invaluable tool for logistics, which can logistically benefit greatly from knowing the exact whereabouts of any product during any point of time. The second most praised characteristic of blockchain is the elevated level of security, making changes to its information nearly impossible once recorded on any device. This is only possible due to the substantial number of separate devices constituting the system and the usage of cryptographic security tools, making both securities and any other data decentralized. Lastly, the third benefit is reducing costs and speeding up transactions due to the elimination of a substantial body of support such as banks, clearinghouses, or brokers.

However, there are also benefits that are not purely operational in nature. One of them is the potential for a new business to appear due to such technology's development. In this case, businesses will actually create applications and services on the blockchain, such as smart contracts or dApps. This is a blockchain-powered application that automatically performs transactions once the status of one of the parties changes according to the rules set by their developers.

The Potential of Decentralized Models and Peer-to-Peer Transactions

Blockchain technology facilitates the transition towards decentralized models and, as a result, enables peer-to-peer transactions. Namely, most existing business models involve a central authority to regulate nodes, enforce rules, and process transactions. In a decentralized system, control is given to all parties interested in the operation of a company, i.e., those who are interacting with one another. This makes blockchain-based systems more efficient and autonomous. In cases where contracts between two entities are due, relies on a blockchain system make sure that transactions are processed and recorded by a pre-existing network of both in real-time, as a result of this mechanism, the trust is implicit and does not need to be established with a central authority. In the case of finance, the notion is referred to as Decentralized Finance as it eliminates the need for depending on banking institutions. DeFi, which implies tracking goods' origin or patients' medical history, and business transactions operate on a systemual basis, reduces waste and productivity when two parties interact directly. There are numerous implications of this feature.

On the one hand, P2P transactions eliminate third parties in most interactions and allow users to trade and make payments directly to one another. This aspect of the blockchain lowers costs, waste, and time when it comes to P2P transactions. The provision of cryptocurrencies as payment adds a unique aspect to the system as it is not limited to a geographical area. For instance, mushers grudging to rely on banks or those reluctant to work by visiting the space can make transactions using the internet. On the other hand, this feature provides blockchain with certain applications as any two parties can interact. In case of finance, DeFi applications can also function in regional or national markets if the entire transaction involves two parties.

In general, P2P interactions are a double-edged sword. When banks and other third parties are removed from the equation, the cost of transactions transfers to entities that must invest in proper equipment to facilitate exchanges or the security of the system. In addition, payments between two parties run along a regional or national trade system and might not be well-recorded or even ignored. In other words, operations continue to function in real-world circumstances and blockchain is affected accordingly.

Case Studies of Blockchain-Based Companies Like Ethereum, Ripple, and Filecoin

Some blockchain-based companies show the power of decentralized technology, introducing it in specific cases to create new value and disrupt traditional industry. Three examples of such companies are Ethereum, Ripple, and Filecoin; these all companies invented new blockchain-based platforms to solve business problem. Ethereum is probably the most famous blockchain platform after Bitcoin. It proposed the new concept of smart contracts, which are contracts coded into the blockchain that define the rules and consequences of the agreement. Smart contracts create decentralized applications (dApps) that run without the need of intermediaries. Ethereum blockchain is used for a variety of purposes, from decentralized finance and exchanges to digital art marketplaces (NFTs). Its application to different problems showed the possible purpose of blockchain as a platform of creating decentralized applications. Ripple is another blockchain-based company which has quite a significant disturbances in the financial services industry. Its platform is based on blockchain and was created to make cross-border payments fast and cheap. While traditional ways of making such payments often include a multitude of intermediaries and several days of processing, transferring money with Ripple's platform based on blockchain is more efficient. It is used by banks in the United Kingdom and Japan. Ripple showed possible implementation with blockchain, which could make some cases of businesses cheaper. Filecoin is another example of using blockchain for creating a new kind of business. Filecoin is a decentralized storage network, where people have to rent out free space on their hard drives and earn some money in cryptocurrency. The network uses blockchain to record information about the sellers, providing them with the opportunity to store their files based on the data storage owners. There are other blockchain implementations in business, but these cases show the variety of possible business models. The companies use blockchain to solve a particular business problem.

How Entrepreneurs Can Explore Blockchain for New Business Opportunities

Blockchain is an innovative technology that provides numerous opportunities for entrepreneurs willing to introduce innovative mechanisms and develop new business models. The technology has already proven its flexibility and effectiveness, offering diverse applications, while as it continues to develop, more opportunities emerge. This paper will present several strategies how entrepreneurs can explore blockchain applications for their businesses.

Initially, entrepreneurs will have to investigate how blockchain can resolve problems existing in their field. For instance, it can be effective in industries that require a high level of transparency, security, and efficiency for transactions or data. Entrepreneurs should also consider areas where there is a need for trust between the transacting parties or where the brokers create additional expenses and complexities, as blockchain can help to remove the element of trust or replace the unnecessary middlemen. As of now, the technology has the potential to disrupt supply chain management, healthcare, real estate, and finance. In these fields, transactions are complex and include multiple participants. In addition, often the data has to be updated frequently, and this can also be automated with blockchain technologies. At the same time, entrepreneurs will need to establish recreation of the needed infrastructure, which might include developing a blockchain platform or cooperating with an existing one.

Another possibility is considering tokenizing some of the rights or assets of the business. Tokenization is a process of creating digital tokens that represent a digital version of assets or rights of the company, the ownership of which can be exchanged. This way of functioning will allow for increasing data liquidity and ease of exchange. Overall, the entrepreneurs will benefit from better control over their assets. However, the process is still in the experimental phase, and it may raise some legal issues.

Another possibility is to create a decentralized application that does not need banks or other service providers. For example, such an application can be developed within the field of finance. Decentralized finance projects allow people to lend, borrow, or exchange digital assets without the need of banks. Overall, a decentralized application created with Ethereum will allow entrepreneurs to get rid of expensive service providers.

There are also several legal barriers. Even though the technology promises numerous benefits, in many instances it still lacks a supportive legal framework. The entrepreneurs should keep track of current legislation and make sure their activities are compliant with state rules on data protection or such issues as security or securities. Another important point is that blockchain was initially created to be collaborative, and thus the entrepreneur needs to build a collaboration network. The adoption of blockchain as a solution to certain problems requires the coordinated effort of multiple stakeholders. Overall, entrepreneurs should investigate blockchain to generate ideas for using it to reorganize the existing business structure or develop a new model altogether.

Chapter 10: Lean Startup Methodology and Agile Business Models

In the modern start-up and entrepreneurship environment, the Lean Startup principles and Agile methodology are two of the most vital frameworks for creating and elevating a business. Both approaches are characterized by flexibility, efficiency, and customer orientation, allowing businesses to maneuver quickly, reduce waste, and enhance their products or services. Constructed by Eric Ries, the primary idea of lean startup focuses on "building a business through a series of experiments designed to test assumptions and develop customer learning as quickly as possible". Therefore, at its core, a lean startup implies launching a certain product or service in the form of an MVP that is the most basic version of an idea that can still offer the value to customers. This product reaches users and provides real-world feedback, which allows entrepreneurs to understand what should be done and change the original idea without burdensome investments of time or money. The fast-cycle loop of building a product, measuring its success, and learning is the central aspect of a lean startup that is repeated constantly to bring the end product closer to users' demands. An Agile methodology is another approach that can be used to describe lean startups. It is a basic aspect of Software Engineering that is applicable to all industries and implies the use of iterative and planning-driven tools. Therefore, it predefines a shorter development cycle known as a sprint where the team can focus on certain parts of a product. Then, this product is tested, adjusted, and eventually improved. Agility is facilitated by the cooperation, communication, responsiveness, and flexibility of the teams involved. Hence, both Lean Start-up and Agile methodologies imply the importance of testing, learning the real experiences of customers, and changing quickly without committing to ideas that were proved to be wrong.

How to Create, Validate, and Pivot Business Models Quickly

The lean startup approach is distinct because it uncouples risk management from waste prevention, focusing on creating and validating business models in a fast and resource-efficient way. The approach relies on the notion of the MVP, which forms the base for the validation of a model. It is typically developed from the entrepreneur's hypotheses – usually, one about the problem to be solved – and serves as a means of testing them, though not a final product yet.

Indeed, minimal here refers not to the quality of the product but the extent of the development – the MVP only contains enough features for solving the problem or adding other value to the customer. This does not mean that the business idea behind it is necessarily simple, but it is important that only its most essential parts are implemented in the MVP. It is then launched, and the entrepreneur sees whether any interest in it will be shown by the early adopters. If the testing turns out to have been unsuccessful, such feedback can reveal what aspect is misjudged – the product itself, the target audience, or the business model. Validation of a business model is achieved through the interactions, as well as the reactions, of the real customers; in order to measure them, several KPIs can be used, such as user retention rates, conversion rates, time of use, and user response time.

Such multiple quantitative indicators can help draw a picture of the product's demand and the quality of one's initial judgements on it. The results provide a basis for deciding what to do next – either continue working along the lines of one's current idea or make a pivot. This is the term that represents the other method by which the lean startup and agile methodologies deal with the risks, and it is almost as central. A pivot is a radical change in direction that is still in touch with the basis of the preceding model and serves as a structured way to test a new hypothesis. It can concern the product, as in cases of Webvan or Apple, who had to completely overhaul their value proposition, or target audience, as in worse-case examples of YouTube earnings dropping and then getting saved as a general video hosting platform. Such changes can be large or small, though it is usually the larger ones that create the most value and it is important to be cultured and timely about them – making the pivot at the right moment.

Case Studies of Companies Like Dropbox, Zappos, and Slack

Many successful companies were built on lean startup and agile methodologies, proving that these approaches could lead to growth and prosperity. Dropbox, Zappos, and Slack are three companies that have achieved success. Early on, founder Drew Houston didn't immediately build a product like Dropbox. Instead, he made a simple video to prove that his idea was viable. He presented it to the world, and he was pleased that many people liked the idea of Dropbox. Earlier, he discovered how to test a marketing idea without spending time on product development. Houston was inspired by excitement and began to develop a product and create a file that can be shared. This approach allowed Dropbox to create a unique product that resolved real issues, leading to growth and prosperity. Thus, MVP also has advantages, and it can be useful if a person does not have enough funds for the greatest performance.

The Zappos shoe retailer began its journey with an MVP by taking pictures of shoes and posting them on the internet. Instead of creating an entire e-commerce platform, founder Nick Swinmurn took photos and uploaded them to the site. Many customers began to buy sneakers. Nick Swinmurn took cash and bought shoes at the store and sent it to customers. Thus, Zapposworkers don't need to rent and buy a warehouse and don't need to store shoes in stock. This approach saved money, and Zappos was able to grow. The retailer received feedback that was a Zappos source of strength. Over time, the company grew, attracting a lot of customers and providing better products. Amazon eventually purchased Zappos.

Slack founder Stewart Butterfield and his team developed an internal messaging system for the company's game. Butterfield quickly realized that such a tool was valuable because employees were eager to use it and it made the company more fun. He decided to devote the product to other companies and new users. As a result, Butterfield launched MVP and started using it to make improvements. MVP involved quick changes and user response, allowing Slack to quickly gather many teams worldwide. This was the method used and the success of the product.

Practical Steps for Entrepreneurs to Adopt a Lean and Agile Approach

However, for entrepreneurs, looking to start using the lean and agile approach, there are several practical steps:

Step 1 : Identify the problem;

Step 2 : Hypothesize the solution that is based on data from the first step;

Step 3 : Develop an MVP that consists of the most important features and is very fast to develop;

Step 4 : Launch and test the MVP, based on the data received from the previous step, decide whether to persist or pivot.

Step 5 : Improve or iterate.

Step 6. Repeat everything over and over again.

There are several important points to consider when using the agile and lean methodology.

Firstly, in the first step, an entrepreneur should first formulate the problem that his future business is going to solve based on which he will be able to come up with a reasonable hypothesis. This hypothesis should meet certain requirements. Firstly, it should be scientific. In other words, the hypothesis should rely on some existing data that the entrepreneur already has. Second, the hypothesis should also be falsifiable. In other words, based on the data received from the MVP, the entrepreneur should understand whether the turned out to be correct.

Secondly, the MVP should in any case be fast to develop and to launch. This is one of the lean startup methodology's principles. The key purpose of the MVP is to test the data that the company already has. It is not supposed to spend months or even years to develop an MVP.

In addition to that, another important requirement for using the lean startup and agile methodologies is a focus on a user need. One of the cornerstone principles of the lean startup methodology is always staying tuned to what the customers really need.

Chapter 11: Crowdsourcing and Collaborative Business Models

One of the powerful tools used in modern business for innovation or funding is crowdsourcing. Crowdsourcing is referred to as the practice of obtaining ideas, services, or funding from a large group of people, mainly from the internet. This concept has revolutionized dozens of companies and entrepreneurs who struggled with solving problems, creating products, or raising capital. By using this tool, entities can access the wisdom and abilities of a particularly large, often global group of people that no single central authority or adequate staff could provide. Crowdsourcing is an advanced innovative technology that suggests new forms of achieving some results that could not have been achieved more significantly, more expensive, or simply impossible to obtain in traditional forms.

In terms of innovation, the power of crowdsourcing lies in the ability of "harnessing the distributed knowledge and creativity of a large crowd". Some industries are innovatively intensive; to remain competitive and develop new products, high levels of intellectual and innovative activity are required. Crowdsourcing is an excellent tool in such cases because external experts or ordinary people who have no connection to the company or industry may look at the problem and suggest ways to solve it from a new, unusual angle. Those who offer ideas may well have a different life experience, and they might see what the company's employees do not see. In the production of such industries, companies often have to deal with the endless repetition of hackneyed and already ineffective methods for designing or creating products. From the outside, people do not work in one industry all the time and, looking at the problem, can offer fresh rather than already well-worn ways.. In terms of funding, crowdsourcing has vast potential and allows the public direct fundraising instead of receiving a bank loan. Fundraising sites offer the service called crowdfunding, under which start-ups are forced to seek funding from ordinary people on a massive scale, who are ready to donate their contribution or make shares in return. Traditional means of obtaining means are restored in comparison with venture capital or a loan in the bank. For some companies, bank loans are suitable and acceptable when they have collateral, while in the absence of it, no bank would take the risk and give such a company a loan. The same goes for venture capital funds that are willing to take a stake only when a company has a sufficiently developed and tested product. Sites for fundraising are essential to obtain the necessary funds and if they are successful, then over time, primarily consumers have a ready rationale in the form of wholesale purchases to develop and move to the extended model of selling. Crowd-based platforms to give money and validate ideas give everyone the ability to check the demand of customers before moving to active sales. Thus, the critical power of crowdsourcing is to provide companies or entrepreneurs new opportunities in the form of many people, from potential contributors to partners to funders, stakeholders, and customers.

Case Studies of Companies Like Kickstarter, Wikipedia, and Waze

A number of companies have employed crowdsourcing to become market leaders or at least some of the most successful establishments. As a result, the title concept has proven its versatility and efficacy. Three highly successful businesses, namely Kickstarter, Wikipedia, and Waze, have made use of different forms of crowdsourcing to achieve success. Kickstarter is particularly notable because it allowed both to utilize crowdsourcing and gave rise to a viable business model in the process. Established in 2009, the company now allows entrepreneurs to attempt to fund their startups, accept donations in exchange for rewards in ten to eight weeks, film makers, musicians, designers of gadgets and games, and so on. of thousands of profitable projects, and the site has made it easier to find financial support. In many ways, it defines the reward system: first, the business owners are encouraged to make an appealing offer, and second, donators are urged to not give money to investors they do not intend to. In addition, it made the coverage of a vast range of businesses more democratic and allowed them all to test project ideas before incurring the costs of production. Wikipedia, in turn, leveraged the knowledge of large numbers of people to build its product. Founded in 2001, the website continues to be developed by volunteers who write, edit, and refine articles and contributions. Despite the concerns that this means the content is untrustworthy from a factual standpoint, Wikipedia has developed a system of moderators and cites its sources on the site. The company has also proven that people can work with each other to create and sustain huge complex systems with relatively minimal administrative intervention. Waze uses crowdsurcing swimming to receive accurate traffic and road information in real-time. It was already a well-established establishment when it was bought by Google in 2013 but still works well as an example of crowdsourcing in the service industry or technology. Let them know if there are any road construction works, accidents, or traffic jams on the road. The company's navigation system crowdsources these data and provides maps as up-to-date as no other. Both offer a fairly definitive explanation of how crowdsourcing can be leveraged, and none of them overlap, so they should be perfectly valid.

How to Build a Community and Leverage Crowds for Growth

The key to any crowdsourcing initiative is a supportive and committed community. A properly motivated crowd can not only fuel the collection of ideas and insights but can also support the promotion of the project or provide funding. However, as all crowdsourcing projects have unique purposes, their communities should also be treated in their specific way. For business and entrepreneurship, it means that several approaches should be combined, including the development of value proposition, constant engagement, recognition, and clear defined purpose.

The first step in building such a community is to define the purpose of a project. The objectives should be transparent, and the reasons for participation should be clear to people. No crowdsourcing initiative will be successful among contributors if they see that their involvement does not matter or they get no clear benefits from it. As soon as the purpose is defined, the crowd should be constantly engaged through feedback collection, regular updates and recognitions. To achieve these purposes, several communication instruments can be used, including social media, newsletters, or other platforms that are popular among users. Also, they can be encouraged to interact among themselves: for example, wicked problems that require solutions can be shared between users, and the dialog can be promoted in the comment sections. However, the main condition is to constantly inform the users about the results of their efforts. Businesses apply these strategies through regular reports on their progress to those, who finance them. Crowdfunding platforms also inform the donors about the objectives reached, and businesses that gather raw ideas through social media also inform their contributors about the ways their ideas were implemented. Another approach to engage contributors is to incentivize them through rewards, recognitions, or gamified contests. For instance, people who share most ideas can be advanced on a virtual leaderboard or be given special "devotee" or "enthusiast" badges.

Practical Tips for Implementing Crowdsourcing in Business Strategies

Crowdsourcing is the process that can benefit many businesses and entrepreneurs. However, it should be noted that implementing this concept in your business strategy and follow a specific approach to align the implementation with desired objectives. There are several practical tips for every entrepreneur or a business' owner who is considering using crowdsourcing as part of their business operations:

1.Identify your goals. As with any other initiative, it is important to know what you wish to achieve. Depending on the exact type of crowdsourcing as well as the facilitation technique, you may want to source new ideas, build software or hardware applications, or receive donations to fund your business. These aspects should be defined precisely and according to the specific scope, such as the desired quantity of innovative ideas or the amount of funding.

2.Select the right platform. There are many existing platforms for entrepreneurs and businesses to use for crowdsourcing the funds for their businesses. Popular crowdfunding platforms are Kickstarter and Indiegogo. If you are looking to crowdsource designs for your element, you may choose 99designs. However, if the business' owner is looking to gather data for their company using the crowd, they should search for other platforms that focus on this specific type of crowdsourcing.

3.Communicate with contributors. Every business that is interested in using crowdsourcing should have a communication plan. The company must keep in touch with contributors, inform them of the updates and planned actions, and ask for the specific types of assistance. Regular updates and calls to action ensure that contributors view the situation not as passive agents but as members of a community that they want to help.

4.Use the data and the assistance provided. Perhaps the most important aspect of any of these ideas is the fact that the companies use the data, design, ideas, or funding provided. If the founders choose not to follow their plans because they believe they found a better way, this information should be conveyed to the contributors.

5.Be accountable. Companies that use crowdsourcing to fund should be responsible for managing the funded funds. If significant deviance from the original plan occurs and the company cannot deliver the promised result, the involved parties should discuss the issue. Being responsible not just to the customers but to the crowds is vital when the transaction amount is significant.

Using these ideas, one can safely implement an adequate and business-aligned crowdsourcing process. The examples of popular companies that began by tapping into the crowd resources demonstrate the potential benefits of the approach: Wikipedia, Waze, and Oculus Rift all started via crowdfunding, with empowered individuals who perceived clear goals and knew what was required from them.

Chapter 12: Leveraging Ecosystems and Strategic Partnerships

In the era of today's hyper-connected global economy, businesses do not anymore operate on their own but rather thrive as part of ecosystems composed of interconnected players. A business ecosystem "describes the network of companies, suppliers, distributors, customers, competitors, and other stakeholders that are involved in the delivery of a specific product or service through both competition and cooperation". On the one hand, the process of ecosystem formation supports the success of the businesses participating in it as it allows them to address the challenges involved in adjusting to the constantly changing landscape. On the other hand, innovation develops as part of business ecosystems as well. It involves, first of all, synergy, but it also encourages cooperation and sharing of responsibility among the ecosystem's members.

In fact, companies involved in business ecosystems often share resources and knowledge and explore new technologies and approaches that they could not develop reinforced on their own. Hardware manufacturers, for instance, build a functioning relationship with software developers and service providers, then teaming up to introduce an integrated solution into the market. Therefore, business ecosystems stimulate innovation by enhancing product offerings and catering to the most recent changes and trends in the market. At the same time, business ecosystems create an environment in which companies find it easier to experiment and iterate. As the industries continue to be disrupted by the swiftly changing technology and market trends, business ecosystems ensure that resident businesses can respond promptly. Therefore, in today's environment, where innovation is essential for the continued functioning and success of every enterprise, ecosystems help businesses create a wider pool of resources and opportunities than any single company could if working on its own.

How to Identify and Develop Strategic Partnerships

The process of creating a growing and developing business ecosystem begins with the search and maintenance of the strategic partnerships. Strategic partnerships imply the relations between different organizations that decide to link to attain shared objectives and create value for one another. There is a wide range of forms that such partnership may take – from joint ventures and alliances to supplier relationships and co-development activity. The first step the company has to take while establishing the strategic partnership is to evaluate its own strengths and weaknesses. I.e., one has to realize which of his processes may be enhanced by the means of another agency's efforts, technology, or resources. One of the examples is the collaboration between a high-tech organization and a design form which will guide the former through improving the products' UX design. Another example concerns the agreement between a technology company and a logistics supplier who may optimize the processes of distributing one's products. The crucial thing to remember is that any partnership should be structured around what each party does best. The aim is to develop relations with the companies whose operations are similar to one's strategic objectives, i.e. the partners' operations should help finding the areas where the company may lack something. The second step is to elaborate the collaboration agreement – the relations should be designed in such a way that the companies "want to keep investing in". The mutual benefits for the companies should also be clear from the beginning, whether it is the expansion of the market, access to the intellectual property, or the creation of jointly developed products. Finally, one should always take care of the relations to let them always be productive and allow to remain a successful partner.

Case Studies of Companies Like Apple, Salesforce, and Microsoft

The practices of companies not only reveal the secrets of ecosystems, which may have led to sustainable performance but also allow other organizations to repeat their behavior. The following are three examples of Apple, Salesforce, and Microsoft. The fir Apple develops applications in its vast App Store ecosystem by partnering with thousands of independent developers across the globe. It provides developers with tools, platforms, and delivery channels, partnering with third-party app developers, and offering consumers a wide range of applications. This ecosystem helps Apple's devices, including the iPhone and iPad, to succeed in the ecosystem, while it has made significant progress in bringing its ecosystem to life by partnering with hardware makers, carriers, and content vendors. The ecosystem of Apple is the world 's tech center and one of the most advanced ones.

Secondly, Salesforce is a cloud-based CRM app and an early ecosystem team initiator. Salesforce has created a vast ecosystem of partners, customers, and third-party developers around its AppExchange cloud platform, allowing users to sell applications that are incorporated in Salesforce CRM. This allows vendors to expand their contact platform capabilities while providing support through other businesses to other companies. It worked with small and large businesses to develop industry-specific cloud applications for cloud distribution of complete cloud CRM solutions. Sales forces quickly developed and has stayed ahead of the CRM market due to the exponentially increasing distribution and incentives for its products.

Thirdly, Microsoft has a strong history of ecosystems, such as the Windows operating system the Azure cloud service. Microsoft has developed relationships with other hardware manufacturers, developers of applications, and cloud storage providers that help with data analytics, the implementation of AI algorithms and IoT. The technology giant of Redmond works with small businesses and business worldwide. It's a big and developing asset.

In conclusion, the above three platforms are able to set a good example of partners which could create relationships for ecosystems, expand their markets and have created lasting value by encouraging such networking and accepting the support of others.

Strategies for Building and Nurturing a Business Ecosystem

Building and nurturing a business ecosystem is not an easy task, and doing it correctly involves multiple steps, from finding the right partners to maintaining proper relationships. The following strategies can help businesses create and support a successful ecosystem that will foster innovation and lasting growth.

* Define the value proposition. Any ecosystem should have a clear value proposition that would motivate all of its members to remain and work together. Whether out of creating a platform, a product, or a service, it should clearly benefit not only the business that created it, but also its partners, customers, and any other collaborators, for example, by providing access to new markets, new capabilities, or novel opportunities for joint innovation. A value proposition also helps to identify the right partners, which will be those potentially interested in the solution; it creates a sense of purpose that will support an informal community and motivates to stay when times get tough.

* Foster collaboration and openness. People and organizations that work in ecosystems are generally expected to have access to the benefits of collaboration, that is, to work together, to communicate, and to share information and resources with each other. Encouraging such cooperation can be helped by creating platforms for communication or hosting regular events or meetings. Moreover, all ecosystem members should have chances to influence and improve it, and companies should strive to encourage and accept feedback, opinions, and cooperation requests.

* Invest in technology and infrastructure. Sometimes, a fitting technology or process is all it takes to help an ecosystem function. Tools, platforms, and infrastructure can ease collaboration and more effectively leverage data, shared between the business and its partners. For example, cloud computing platforms can make it easier for partners to interact with your service, while APIs and software development kits will make creating integrations more flexible.

* Adapt the ecosystem. The most useful ecosystems are likely to be those that can adapt to new market conditions, technologies, or customer needs. Being able to recognize and quickly address deficiencies, for example, by adding new partners, adopting new technologies, and accessing new markets, may help the business ensure that the ecosystem will remain useful in the future.

* Create incentives for participation. Ecosystems can be useful only if people are interested in them, and incentives can help ensure that people remain interested in the partnership. Those can be financial

or other rewards or simply new opportunities to grow and explore. It is important to create a system that will be beneficial for all the apter, providing them with incentives to stay.

* Manage relationships. Successfully developing an maintaining an ecosystem requires a company to be actively working with its partners, maintaining communication, and dealing with issues as they arise. It is important to work together to resolve potentially existing sources of tension and to celebrate together any sources of success.

Companies can use of the following strategies to build a successful ecosystem that will bring long-term success and lasting growth. Well-developed ecosystems can facilitate the use of a huge number of different resources and capabilities, creating better opportunities for companies to innovate and expand.

Chapter 13: Sustainability and Circular Economy Models

The circular economy is one of the modern trends for business development. It involves a new approach to the use of resources in contrast to a linear economy with the 'take, make, dispose' model. In a circular economy, resources are reused continuously, and minimized waste with broader use of products. This possibility becomes achievable due to things designed to be durable, reused, remanufactured, and recycled. Implementing a circular economy allows organizations to avoid supply risks and reduce the amount of waste and the costs of waste disposal. They also are able to create new revenue streams due to such offerings as product-as-a-service, remanufacturing and recycling services. While businesses gain a clear profit from implementing a circular economy model, it provides distinctive competitive advantage by supporting long-term customer relations and loyalty. The approach meets the demands of customers who require sustainable practices from modern brands. Thus, it is a way to improve corporate image. Companies that use resources more efficiently are better positioned to avoid the impacts of volatile resources markets and create beneficial conditions for business development. The very concept of a circular economy requires the product design. It makes companies look for alternative ways of manufacturing and logistics. Thus, a way to reduce resources use causes the constant redesign of products and business models. In such a way, organizations that engage in a circular model force to generate more innovations that increase the effectiveness of the process and product quality.

How Sustainability Can Be Integrated into Business Models

The process of integrating sustainability into business models requires more than adopting any number of eco-friendly practices. It is a complete reformation of how value is created, delivered, and captured in such a way that the success of the business corresponds with earth-friendly practices. The main approach to integrating sustainability is by 'welding' responsible practices into each aspect of the value chain, from product design and manufacture to end-of- product life. Designing with an idea to the immediate and ultimate needs of a product's life is critical to integrating sustainability. This can be facilitated by using materials that are either completely biodegradable or recyclable. For instance, when it comes to recycling, glass and metals have no 'downcycling' problems, so they are perfect from this perspective. Additionally, it is important to consider that lightweight products originating from less polluting materials will use fewer resources in the production of 'replacement' goods. Such design decisions can be quite cost-effective, as more of the materials will be reused and there will less need to spend vast resources on the manufacture of a product.

An additional approach to integrating sustainability is applying it to supply chain management. In the creation of products, companies can be encouraged to partner with suppliers who have similar commitments to the creation of sustainable products. Such standards can then be applied to the selection of raw materials which should be mined or produced in such a way that respects the conditions in which people are working and their wider community. Applying energy-efficient practices and thus reducing the number of emissions created during transportation or manufacture will also ensure that companies are adhering to the principles of creating sustainable goods while facilitating operational efficiency. Another approach to this problem is developing circular business models, which are limited only by the creativity of the innovators. For example, products might be marketed as 'product as a service' or through subscription services. In the first case, the company retains the ownership of the product but only leases it 'temporarily' to the customer who benefits from its service while the product is in good condition. When it stops working or becomes dysfunctional, the customer returns it to the company which then has its product serviced and goes selling to other customers. All approaches are supplemented by the cultivation of an environmentally friendly corporate culture, which cab manifest through a company-wide initiative to promote recycling, encourage the widespread use of renewable resources, and others. Most successful companies ensure that their documents and therefore the entire organization's practices are run in a way that minimizes the amount of equipment and therefore money spent on outsourcing. To present a workforce with a set of policies to ensure this, there must be an element of performance measurement, meaning that firms which consider themselves committed to environmental responsibility have set measurable targets for their suppliers. Either through the use of key performance indicators or applicable international standards, the progress of the company must be reported to its stakeholder, from customers to shareholders.

Case Studies of Companies Like IKEA, Tesla, and Loop

Nowadays a number of best practice companies have become pioneers in integrating the circular economy principles into their business models, thus demonstrating that sustainability can go in line with profitability. Among such enterprises are IKEA, Tesla, and Loop, which have adopted a number of circular strategies to decrease waste, lengthen the lifecycles of products, and contribute to a more sustainable future. IKEA, being a well-known furniture retail giant, appears to be a vivid example of a company that adheres to the principles of the circular economy and sustainability. To reduce the environmental footprint of its operations, IKEA commits to using solely renewable and recycled materials for all products by 2030. Furthermore, in line with the circular strategy, the company appeals to customers to return used furniture, which might be recycled or resold. IKEA also produces furniture which is easy to disassemble or repair, therefore facilitating customer's ability to prolong the life of purchased goods. Finally, to satisfy the customers' growing interest in sustainable shopping, IKEA has launched furniture leasing and take-back programs, thus decreasing the amount of waste and resources consumed. Another best practice example to adhere to the principles of sustainability is Tesla, one of the world-leading manufacturers and developers of electric cards. Tesla's business model is focused on making use of sustainable energy and, hence, reducing carbon emissions. At the same time, this approach facilitates the process of electric battery recycling, allowing for the recovery of such materials as lithium, cobalt, and nickel. In the long run, this closed/loop system of the material use optimizes the production of batteries and cuts down the need for mining raw materials. Finally, Loop, a recent innovative enterprise operating within the sphere of elimination packaging waste, arranges for reusable containers with everyday items. The customers purchase the products and have the containers delivered, while after these items are used, they return containers back. The latter are then washed and refilled so that they could be delivered back to the market. The circular model allows cutting down the use of single-packaging and developing a more sustainable consumption pattern. Loop has already established partnerships with a number of best practice brands, such as Procter and Gamble, Unilever, and Nestle, and implemented the model in a number of countries. Thus, IKEA, Tesla, and Loop have become best practice examples of companies integrating sustainability practices in their business models, and their experience can offer a number of valuable insights for future entrepreneurs.

Steps for Entrepreneurs to Build Sustainable and Circular Business Models

Entrepreneurs who are interested in developing sustainable and circular business should concentrate their efforts in these areas by attempting to create long-term value in their ventures while simultaneously attempting to minimize possible environmental repercussions. The following step-by-step plan should help entrepreneurs in such a pursuit.

1. Start with Sustainable Design. One of the most significant first steps is associated with the idea of creating a product or service that would require significantly fewer materials to be successfully implemented. Using natural resources and attempting to design the product to be parted out in the worst possible-case scenario should be the first measure that has to be kept in mind. Entrepreneurs must remember that even at this early stage in the cycle, they should already be thinking about the end of the same cycle.

2. Embrace the Circular Economy Mindset. Establish a business model that is unlike a vast majority of the currently observed variations of the same concept. In a circular business model, entrepreneurs are selling products that were created by using materials seized from the customer in the past. Companies are not selling products but rather value through different services. The best examples of the abovementioned models are those regarding Product-as-a-Service or Take-Back systems implemented by the entrepreneur.

3. Unite with Sustainable Partners. Partners and suppliers play an important role in any industry. When entrepreneurs want to develop an eco-friend business model, they have to work with

suppliers, manufacturers, and distributors who think just the same. Entrepreneurs have to acquire eco-friendly materials and supplies so the whole supply chain should be a part of the created sustainable business.

4. Efficient but Green. Each entrepreneur wants his company to be successful, which is why they should reduce the emissions and waste of their company. By installing solar roof panels, entrepreneurs can reduce energy waste. At the same time, modern technology helps to create efficient logistics. Insights into the abovementioned measures would help entrepreneurs in the business and any other type of operation that is performed.

5. Educate and Mobilize Customers. Another vital aspect of a truly circular business model is its customer. Far too many customers still show disregard for environmental concerns and, as a result, businesses can hardly evolve the necessary set of values. By establishing a circular business and implementing various measures, entrepreneurs should also teach their customers about benefits of the product/service that was created and encourage the same customers to be involved in the alternations of the products, such as taking back a faulty product and renting a product by representatives of the same company.

6. Measure and Communicate Your Efforts. Entrepreneurs, as well as everyone else, have to be transparent in their actions. They should know that all their efforts will not be for naught if they can show how well they performed and all the wipes they managed to make. Customers and investors alike have to know the results of the latter and they should have been previously stated goals. By following the steps and utilizing technologies, entrepreneurs can share their contribution to the environment that will become a part of the brand credit.

7. Continue to Innovate. Business is a volatile area. What was good a few years ago may already be insufficient for reaching success. Entrepreneurs always have to be on the lookout for innovative ideas, devices, tools, and methods related to energy-efficient technologies or sustainable initiatives. By doing so, they can still remain up to date in the era when such information changes rapidly.

In the end, people should always know that they can develop the most sustainable business in the world but it can still fail without regard for anything. In order to succeed, the source or service has to be useful and, at first, by useful, people usually associate cheap or good in quality. By following the steps and given insights, entrepreneurs will be able to build a business that is successful and respectful to the earth just as the customers. They will also be able to gather more and more interest as the number of such businesses is increasing in the modern world.

Chapter 14: The Role of Corporate Culture in Business Model Innovation

Corporate culture is the set of informal rules and beliefs that contribute to the operation of a company. Culture may be both enabling to the company and disabling innovation. Culture has a lot of impact on companies; it defines the way in which employees conduct themselves and the way they interact with each other. Also, it is the key for developing ideas and fostering innovation.

The basic difference between the two is that an innovation-enabling culture focuses on promoting new ideas and supports testing new things to improve efficiencies. However, a disabling culture imposes regular and routine practices and hinders innovation by discouraging innovation and only using existing ideas to limit risk taking, while encouraging routine practices, disciplining failures, and using performance appraisals to limit rewards for creativity. Innovation-enabling culture serves as a valuable tool that helps share the creative process and incentives implemented in the company. Encouraging innovation means creating a set of rules and opportunities to reward creativity.

To my mind, a culture-enabling innovation mailing is connected with some aspects that include lack of punishment for sharing ideas, used mechanism of getting feedback, as well as rewarding and recognition means. The most influential of them is reward and recognition for creativity through a range of innovative ideas and contribution to the overall success of the company. Rewarding should come up with additional financial support and career advancement, performance review skill, and contribution in innovation process. To sum up, corporate culture plays a major role in the sphere of innovation, and implementation of mechanisms to enable the culture is essential.

Developing a Culture That Embraces Risk and Encourages Creativity

Making a corporate culture be innovative is not a one-man job. For that, the company needs to suppress the inclination to possess staff and instead allow creative and sometimes risky undertakings to be encouraged. It becomes immediately self-evident that a coherent 'innovative culture' could not come about if a company is afraid it would ultimately lose the staff to competitors. This type of work is inherently volatile and demands a dynamic organization with corresponding manpower attitudes. To fail is the most meaningful milestone a company would have precisely because it has an innovative culture that allows their staff some liberties.

To begin with, the company should introduce free-thinking and market-related education in the staff. The present-day business world is changing so fast that what any one individual learned at a university five years ago is already obsolete. In addition, Google and the West Coast are legendary for hiring quirky 'specialists' with specific knowledge in whatever area they hire them in. The upshot is that the staff should acquire a set of personality traits comprising a 'growth mindset', which would be attained through training. A fixed mindset claims talents are a given, while a growth mindset presupposes they are to be learned. A company develops a growth mindset within itself should view challenges as opportunities to develop rather than threats. This goes to explain that an indisputable fact of today's engineering world is that any discovery is 80–90% some failure. How many companies would be willing to take 80–90% of their salaries or bonuses? Neither does failure feel good, but one can stomach it because they understand it is merely part of the process. One of the areas ripest for improvement is group work. Its efficiency is positively affected by communications and data compatibility. The most innovative companies make sure all the information that exists within the companies actually moves freely. Randomness seems to be an insuperable obstacle to implementing such a solution. That is not always the case since sometimes it is so re-foundable and easy to implement your staff will be the first to suggest it. For that, one should allow them to communicate and, indeed, in such a way that would allow the unusual employees to communicate with those unusual differently from them. Thus, it stands to reason that innovation demands losing some possession of the staff by introducing them to the culture allowing free communication and mutual assistance. Furthermore, the staff needs to acquire a training set of the personality traits comprising a 'growth mindset'. Lastly, a company needs to foster a culture where failure is allowed and even desired.

Being a leader in a company with a culture of innovation means removing some of one's own importance. Yet if a leader does indeed show more readiness to accept being redundant and foolish than his employees without losing their enthusiasm, they could consider taking the definitive step to attain the status a leader should boast. The staff will only think of taking an original well-thought-out and innovative measure when it has a certain work ethic. If a leader allows failure and supports those daring fate around them and rewards their efforts at having failed even where he/she knows they have failed, the staff will usually introduce him to something really exceptional!

Case Studies of Companies Like Google, 3M, and Zappos

It is widely known that there are many companies that became widely known for their innovative culture. Many of them have been achieving great success in the business, and that is why there are many valuable lessons that can be learned from them. There are such examples of companies that used to be unsuccessful but then due to changing their innovational strategy have managed to achieve success. Google, Zappos, and 3M are examples of companies where innovative company culture has brought success and helped to generate the most profitable brand in the world.

One of the most widely known rules of Google is their 20% time. According to this rule, a company allows its employees to spend 20% of their workweek on projects that are not directly connected with their job responsibilities. It is likley that this policy has generated some of the most successful products of Google company. During these 20 % of spare time, some of the top products were developed, such as Gmail and Google News. The other amzing feature of Google's innovation culture is the culture of experimentalism. Moreover, Google guys tend to base their conclusions and decisions on data. Moreover, there is almost no value in waiting for someone to take a risk because the experiment is just part of the process. Another important detail to mention is that Google's innovational culture is based especially on encouraging employees to ask "what if" questions.

3M's innovation culture is likely to be the same as Google's because they have a policy that is called the 15% rule. 3M allows its employees to spend 15% of their time on what they want to do. In addition, the other rule is to get into hot water, otherwise, they will never discover anything. In general, 3M's innovation culture is showing that when it comes to creating a process in a company, it is more important to never try to make a mistake. It is important to cut a process in a safe environment and never be afraid of failurs. It is important to make leaders in the company to understand it because if they want employees to create great products, they have to allow them not to be afraid of making mistakes. As, as a result, they will pay to have only one Post-it instead of thousands of useless products. It is important for a compa to be innovative so that the employees believe in their success as well as support all their initiative. They must be both supported in the company and provided with all the resources they need. They should always take into account the number of successes and achievements that will benefit from them as from any other experiments and trials.

When it comes to a Zappos company, it has managed to cultivate an innovative corporate culture by focusing on employees' interest and happiness. One of the other main features is that they have built an organizational culture. They are trying to do the same with regard to the working process so that the employees can take the initiative and make decisions easily without any hurry. In addition, the company's main values such as "Be a little weird"? or "Take a chance" mean that the employees are encouraging heir employees to think productively and neither the company's employees p nor the dress code, nor creatively. As a result, Zappos has not only become a great brand that has managed to achieve a very strong position on the market. The example of the company is showing that if one company really invests in its organizational culture, it will benefit from innovations and other advantages.

Practical Strategies for Cultivating a Culture of Innovation

There are a number of practical strategies companies interested in building a culture of innovation could use to start the process. The first step involves the focus on the role of leadership, which means that senior executives must actively communicate the significance of innovation as an organizational value. Therefore, leaders need to consistently deliver the message that the company will not succeed without innovative capability. Secondly, organizations should also focus on providing employees with the tools and infrastructure to innovate, which may include offering workshops on creative problem-solving, investing in internal collaboration tools, or, like those empirical companies, creating separate innovation labs. As illustrated by Google and 3M, the practice of facilitating employees' exploration of projects beyond their daily tasks might lead to breakthroughs in new opportunities. Recognizing and rewarding of innovative efforts is no less important, as employees should feel appreciated for their work and realize that the efforts and risks they take are considered significant. Such practices as offering bonuses for successful innovation, as exemplified by QuickTrip, may be used, although companies are also expected to learn from failures and not punish employees for unsuccessful ideas. Finally, a number of practices could be used to support the development of a culture where employees regardless of their positions are encouraged and enabled to collaborate. In particular, companies could create regular brainstorming sessions, hackathons, or innovation challenges where different employees can get together and offer and try to develop creative solutions. It is also important to prioritize communication as an organizational value so that individuals feel comfortable with sharing their thoughts, concerns, and suggestions. It could be argued that, in order to succeed, timely and clear communication should be enculturated and become a part of such emerging cultural contexts as verbal, possessions of discourse, and physical morale.

Chapter 15: Anticipating the Future: Business Models in 2030

The pace at which the business terrain is changing is unprecedented due to advances in technology and changes in consumer behavior. As a result, despite being in the middle of the digital age, it is quite apparent that future trends and disruptions to various industries are an inevitable incident. There is no doubt that such disruptions will be both advantageous and disadvantageous. However, the vital thing to note is that with these disruptions, they are going to force change across the industry domains, meaning that most if not all businesses must rethink how they run their daily lives. As such, AI and automation is the most significant trend that will disrupt how businesses run their activities. Across the board, machine learning, predictive analytics, robotic process automation, and other similar artificial intelligence sciences will have an impact in industries such as healthcare, finance, retail, and manufacturing. As a result of these changes, processes within these industries will become more streamlined, efficient, and more personal in the way they run their activities. As it is, with these changes come disruptions by AI-powered machines, which will perform tasks previously only possible by a human being.

In addition to this, other trends are more likely to continue as they have already started transforming organizations and how they do their activities. One such trend is the reduction of office presence through virtual team technologies. As was previously the norm, more and more companies have begun adopting a hybrid office setup where employees can either work in the office or the safety of their homes. Changes are already happening due to remote work, and with office space becoming a lesser priority, company strategies and modalities for operation will change. In the same manner, industry culture and the hiring of new employees is going to change as companies adapt to working in a more remote manner than previously was the case. Finally, these trends will coincide with the significant trend of sustainability and companies that do not adopt workable models of sustainability including the circular economy model will face increased disruption as their products or services become unpopular with both consumers and investors.

Finally, the decentralization of industries is also another likely source of disruption as the general economy continues to transition to a digital economy, with DeFi, cryptocurrencies, and blockchain technologies leading the way.

The Role of Emerging Technologies Like Quantum Computing and the Metaverse

Two of the emerging technologies that can help to completely disrupt industries are quantum computing and the metaverse. While both are still extremely early in their development, the potential benefits they offer can lead to new business and market opportunities in a few years. Quantum computing can solve problems that are beyond classical computers at speeds none have ever seen before. The number of applications that can benefit from such a technology is virtually endless. It can completely transform the ways some industries operate and open many possibilities that are not currently feasible. The various businesses that rely on vast amounts of data, such as the healthcare, energy, logistics, and financial industries, can be revolutionized by quantum computing. For example, pharmaceutical companies can use the technology to more easily model molecular interactions and expedite the discovery of new drugs. Logistics companies can make their supply chains much more efficient by simultaneously solving multiple optimization problems that used to be impossible before quantum computing. The financial industry can also benefit from quantum computing's ability to quickly analyze vast amounts of data to predict changes in market trends and plan out risk management strategies.

The metaverse is a digital space that people can access as an extension and an enhancement of their reality, using augmented reality, virtual reality, and digital spaces. People can interact with and among themselves and with the entities present in the metaverse. It can be used for many new applications that have not been developed so far. Some companies are already exploring it as a new space where different products and services can be marketed, bought, and sold. For example, retailers can create virtual shopping malls where customers can see 3D models of items and see how they look from all sides. The technology and information industries can use it for entertainment and education purposes, such as interactive virtual reality tours through important historic sights. The metaverse is already being used in various ways and can be used to gain advantages in terms of customer relationships and marketing strategies. Businesses that are able to recognize this change and develop new approaches in terms of how to use it can greatly benefit in the future. Of course, both quantum computing and the metaverse present many technical challenges and can be difficult to develop. They also come with their own management, ethical, and legal problems. It is likely that some types of data can be used in a quantum computing manner only if the data security of quantum computers is greatly improved. The metaverse can also be heavily dependent on software and hardware technologies whose development is held back by economical and other reasons. Businesses that are able to properly address and plan for these challenges will likely be the leaders of these important emergent technologies.

Preparing for the Future: How to Remain Adaptable and Forward-Thinking

In the rapidly changing world, where new technologies and transformations dictate the rules and reshape industries, businesses should be able to adapt to new conditions. Therefore, preparing for the future of a firm is tightly connected to readiness and the ability to anticipate changes by fostering a forward-thinking mindset. The primary steps on this way are to develop a culture of continuous learning and the corporate-wide acceptance of new trend adoptions.

First, it is essential to note that one of the necessary steps for a future-proof company is to create and develop a culture of continuous learning. While future-ready business should be focusing on the growth and development of employees, who have to become aware of the latest concepts and advancements and be ready to master new technologies and practices, on the same level, leaders should be educated and ready for changes. Therefore, continuously training and education staff and managerial personnel becomes a necessary step for companies.

Second, another aspect of being future-proven is a focus on ready and willing for changes and innovation staff. As seen, in the modern times of rapid transformation, standing still is equal to falling behind other firms, the ability and eagerness to experiment and innovate should be encouraged and practiced across the company. For example, participating in a rewarding system for new ideas sharing may become an essential feature for fostering innovation. In addition, intrapreneurship should become an important part of the company's work, creating the atmosphere of a startup across the firm and supporting the possibility to take risks. As essential is the ability to adapt and experiment, it is important to be ready to use and integrate new technologies. For instance, today, implementation and usage of AI, blockchain, or IoT devices might potentially change the way a firm operates and the number of potential customers it can reach.

Finally, as a technique for staying future-ready, scenario planning should be mentioned. The feature of this methodology is that firms can predetermine several potential outcomes by defining scenarios in advance and identifying the way they will respond to them. It helps stay more concentrated and possible threats and have the response plan ahead of time. Therefore, considering the number of opportunities and the rate technologies develop, the use of scenario planning might be applicable in many cases.

Encouragement for Entrepreneurs to Experiment, Iterate, and Innovate

For entrepreneurs, the future is intertwined with numerous opportunities to invent new, disruptive business models that would redefine industries. However, business success in the era of rapid changes will require a sufficient agreement to experiment, iterate, and innovate. Taking an incremental approach to product design and development is key to creating both value for customers and competitiveness in a long-term perspective. One of the most successful approaches towards becoming an entrepreneur and winning a niche in the market is to adopt a lean startup methodology focused on experimenting and iterating as the primary ways of creating sustainable value.

Hence, the first key recommendation for entrepreneurs is to resort to rapid experimentation and iterative approaches to product development. Instead of wasting four years making a perfect product that customers will not need or accept on the market, entrepreneurs are encouraged to design a minimal viable product and put this product to use among real customers. This approach facilitates a rapid cycle of learning from customer feedback and correcting the product based on this feedback. It is critical to realize that product development and iteration should be driven by data, rather than by false assumptions about product performance. As a result, the data-driven nature of entrepreneurship is one of the primary factors responsible for long-term success. Entrepreneurs are encouraged to take risks and explore what mechanisms might not have been previously perceived as possible.

Finally, since they future is related to the emergence of the new business ecosystem, entrepreneurs should also be able to cooperate. A well-developed network of partners, mentors, and business relations will ensure that entrepreneurs can find the missing resources, information, and organizational support they will need. To connect to a broader entrepreneurial system and connect to people who share these goals and values, I will check out events such as those above and perhaps join an accelerator. In sum, the future is with us, and the opportunities are almost unlimited for those who are ready to experiment and innovate.

Conclusion: Leveraging Disruption for Entrepreneurial Success

At the beginning of the end of our journey exploring the potential of different disruptive business models, it becomes evident that the future of entrepreneurship depends on the ability to innovate and change. Disruption is no longer an abstract concept but a practical and necessary strategy that any business should adopt to outcompete the rivals. The main lessons I may take out of this book is that the greatest opportunities emerge as long as the businesses come up with new habitual approaches, employ cutting-edge technologies, and meet new demands and requirements. For me personally and for the majority of other businesspeople, I assume, one of the most important insights is that one should be aware of the necessity for permanent evolution. The market environment is in a constant state of change driven by technological advancements and the social and economic peculiarities of the world. Business which want to have a leading position in the long run are those that can not only understand this particular reality but also capitalize on it. Innovation is not only about new products and services as it presupposes that value can be delivered in a new way, and the habitual order should be under constant attack to meet the challenges with new, improved strategies and methods. Subscription businesses, platforms, sharing and purposeful businesses are examples of such disruption, and they are only few among many other types and applications that can be counted. The cases examined in the course of our learning process from Netflix and Spotify to Airbnb, Uber, and TOMS Shoes demonstrate that it is possible to make a difference employing these strategies because they are disruptive and alter the rules and paradigms the target audiences and rivals work with.

While there are many variations in business models, it is apparent that there are several general strategies that can help entrepreneurs leverage the power of disruption and be successful. The main lesson is that businesses should foster a culture of innovation. This means that entrepreneurs should strive to build an environment in which risk-taking is encouraged, and employees are empowered to think differently. Innovation often occurs when businesses can iterate and test new business models and sales tactics Therefore, employers should be comfortable making big changes when the situation calls for it. Generally, these affect not only the products that companies sell but also the markets in which they are active. The example of Google shows that by fostering an innovative culture with "Google Day" concept, companies can create new products and platforms that change the industry. 3M also used this technique, allowing employees to spend one day a week working on a new project of their choice, which led to new products, such as Post-It notes.

Another important lesson from this book is that the central role of emerging technology in disruption cannot be overstated. Whether computers, the Internet, smartphones, or, most recently, blockchain, artificial intelligence, the metaverse, and other emerging technologies, having a specific technology as the core of a business model can be hugely advantageous. It is important to note that not only can they often represent an excellent opportunity for how to engage customers, streamline the businesses' operations, or disruptive business models, but they can open up entirely new markets and even change the type of product or service that a business is selling. At the very least, businesses that take advantage of these technologies can lead their industries as the industry future instead of watching the future happen to them. Therefore, the main lesson for entrepreneurs is that they must accept that change is rapid today, and it is not possible to exchange the market contexts all the time. Meaning entrepreneurs who can adapt quickly to major changes related to technology, disruption, and other trends will be the ones who are successful. Therefore, entrepreneurs should be driven to always learn from the market and always be on the hunt for ways to make their product or service better.

The time has come to make a final call to action to all the entrepreneurs interested in reshaping their businesses in such a way as to stay not only afloat but become significant players in the environment of disruption. The overall idea is not to wait for changes and adjust the business to meet the new requirements, but to search for ways these changes could be introduced. The book suggests a few winning models and methodologies to elaborate on; however, it is recommended not to stop here. On the contrary, consider it just a starting point and set a goal of trying something fundamentally new in the business environment.

The present-day environment has become so changeable that only the most durable and flexible business models can survive. Thus, challenge yourself to think about the business in the context of the future market. Naturally, there exist not that many books and articles that go the whole nine yards, offering an extensive range of alternative methodologies and practices. In this order of ideas, it is recommended not to limit oneself to data retrieved from the book. The Innovator's Dilemma by Clayton Christensen as well as the Lean Start-up by Eric Ries will provide you with the necessary background knowledge of the models of innovation. Sure thing, the most profitable source of alternative knowledge will be online courses available on Coursera, edX, or Udacity as well as other platforms. In particular, you might want to try a few TechCrunch or Wired new articles or Harvard Business Review reports on disruption as technology advances. In conclusion, the aforementioned sources will put you in a deliberate position where you will be able to unveil the business. The thing is to do it now, do not wait and ponder the issue later.

About the Author

Alex Wealthfield is a forward-thinking business strategist and author with a passion for uncovering innovative paths to success in the entrepreneurial world. With a background rooted in both personal values and professional excellence, Alex brings a unique blend of spiritual alignment and cutting-edge business insight. In her latest work, "Innovative Business Models: Disruptive Strategies for the Modern Entrepreneur," she delves into the dynamic trends shaping the future of business, offering actionable strategies for entrepreneurs eager to thrive in a rapidly changing world. Alex's expertise lies in fusing traditional wisdom with modern innovation, making her a trusted guide for readers who seek not just success but also meaningful impact in their entrepreneurial journeys.